THE BEST OF KEEPERS –

The Life and Artistry of
DON TALLON

The Cricket Publishing Company
Cherrybrook
NSW Australia

First published in Australia in 2000
The Cricket Publishing Company
for the Bradman Foundation
    under the imprint
    Bradman Library

© Philip Derriman 2000
Distributed by   The Cricket Publishing Company
                  14 Barry Street
                  Cherrybrook
                  NSW 2126
                  Email: cardwell@acay.com.au

National Library of Australia
Cataloguing-in-Publication data

Derriman, Philip, 1943 –
The Best of Keepers – The Life and Artistry of Don Tallon
Bibliography
ISBN 09597045 90

1.   Don Tallon
2.   Cricket – Australia – Biography
3.   Cricket players – Australia – Biography
4.   Wicket Keepers

Cover design: Luke Causby
Book design: Ronald Cardwell
Front cover: Don Tallon keeping in England – 1948.
Back cover: Various cigarette and trade cards depicting Don Tallon.

Set in New Baskerville.

Printed and Bound in Australia by
Greenwood Press
62 Arundel Street, Glebe N.S.W. 2037

Greenwood Press

CONTENTS

FOREWORD

By W.A. BROWN

A glance through the records shows that the first occasion I shared the cricket field with Don Tallon was a Sheffield Shield match in Sydney that began on the last day of 1934. I played for NSW and he, of course, for Queensland. My main memory of this match is being run out for 89 when I backed up too far and a drive by my opening partner, Jack Fingleton, was deflected by the bowler into the stumps. But I have no recollection at all of Don Tallon, who stood behind me in both innings. He was an 18-year-old boy then (I was a mature 22) and I suppose I scarcely knew who he was. Eighteen months later, however, when I moved to Queensland, the state of my birth, I began to hear a lot about Don Tallon. Indeed, Tallon was the talk of the town in Brisbane. He was still only 20 years old, yet Queenslanders were convinced that he was something special, that he was destined to be one of the game's stars.

In this, of course, they were completely correct, even if Don's rise to stardom was to be delayed by the war. Don Tallon was certainly something special. I am not living in the past when I say that he did things better and faster behind the stumps than anyone I have seen to date. He performed with a flair which I have not encountered in anyone else: every so often he did things which took your breath away and you would think to yourself, 'Only Tallon could have done that.' It was a kind of inbuilt brilliance which I am quite sure was pure natural talent. No amount of practising could enable anyone else to do the things that Don did.

I was having a drink in the Gresham Hotel in Brisbane when the Australian team for the 1938 tour of England was announced. My delight at being included was mixed with personal disappointment at Don's exclusion. I could not believe he had been left out, for it seemed obvious to me then that he was the best keeper available. I do not know how Don reacted to the news, but I am sure it must have been a terrible let-down for him, but to his great credit he pressed on regardless. It was inevitable he would make the Australian team sooner or later. The pity was that, because of the war, it proved to be much later.

When I think of Don Tallon now, various memories come to mind. He was quite tall, just under six foot, yet he used to fold himself up behind the stumps more tightly than any other keeper I have seen – evidence of his great flexibility. Don did not ever boast about his own achievements (this was one of the things I liked about him) and I never heard him criticise others for their shortcomings. I have a clear recollection of him batting in the nets and striking the ball in that crisp way of his, but I cannot say I ever saw him practise his keeping. No doubt he felt he had enough practice in the middle. I was reminded when reading this book by Philip Derriman that on one occasion Tallon did practise taking the bowling of George Tribe after Don Bradman warned him that Tribe's wrong'un was hard to pick. I can personally vouch for this: Tribe's wrong'un was extremely hard to pick and beat me more than once.

I was also reminded when reading this book that Tallon did have his off days. At times like these he would give an impression of being lackadaisical. It did not happen often but when it did the difference in his performance was so obvious that nobody could help but notice. Having played with him as much as I did, I am quite sure that his stomach ulcers were the cause of those off days. Tallon did not complain about it, but I knew him well enough to know when he was suffering.

I have a clear picture in my mind of Don's keeping, of course: his incredible speed, his flair, and the smooth, unostentatious way he did things. But equally I remember the sharp cricketing mind that lay behind it all. Don was a deep thinker on the game, and his insights were extremely valuable to me when I was captaining Queensland. He might say to me at the end of an over that so-and-so was not bowling well, and I would nearly always be influenced by his advice. Don Tallon did not talk a lot, but whenever he spoke on cricket every word was worth listening to.

I am told this is the first book ever written about Tallon, which is why I am delighted it has been written. It would have been a pity if old players like me who saw Don in action at close quarters and knew how amazingly talented he was had all passed away before someone had tried to chronicle his career. Don Tallon was, as the title of this book suggests, the best of keepers. He was also a very likeable fellow. For both reasons, I respect his memory.

Bill Brown
November, 2000.

ACKNOWLEDGEMENTS

A book of this kind, which relies heavily on first-hand recollections, is necessarily a team effort. Many people were indispensable in its production and none more so than Ronald Cardwell, who not only conceived the idea for it and oversaw its publication but also did much valuable research. In particular, he spoke to Don's widow, Lynda Tallon, his sister Jessie and his two daughters, Catherine and Jane. Fortunately, many of Don Tallon's contemporaries were available to be interviewed, and to those former players who gave of their time to talk about Tallon I offer thanks. I am also grateful to a number of Bundaberg people who allowed me to tap their memories, most notably Noel Wright, Tom Theodore, Percy Stibe, Ian Petherick and Nev Rackemann. Editorial work was carried out by Ronald Cardwell and Colin Lees. Finally, we should all be very grateful to the Bradman Foundation for supporting a book about a player who, being supreme in his field, has always deserved one.

– Philip Derriman, Sydney.

THE AUTHOR

Philip Derriman has been writing on cricket for the *Sydney Morning Herald* for the past 20 years and is the author of numerous books including *The Grand Old Ground, True to The Blue* (a history of the NSW Cricket Association), *Bodyline, The Top 100 & The 1st XI, 80 Not Out* and *Grassy Pitches And Glory Years.* He also compiled two cricket anthologies, *Bat & Pad* and *Our Don Bradman,* and was the editor of the *Australian Cricket Almanac* from 1990 to 1996. In 1984 he went to Queensland to interview Don Tallon for the *Sydney Morning Herald* and was about to arrive in Bundaberg when news came of Tallon's death.

1
THE BEST OF KEEPERS

In early 2000 the Australian Cricket Board appointed 20 selectors, mainly former players and journalists, to choose the best Australian team of the 20th century. When the team was announced with much fanfare at a lunch in Sydney, Ian Healy was found to be the selectors' choice as wicketkeeper – a quite reasonable decision, everyone agreed, considering the magnitude of Healy's achievements. At the time, though, there were some whose minds turned back to another keeper from Queensland, Don Tallon. It was almost 50 years since Tallon retired from big cricket, so few of the selectors could possibly have seen him in action. People who did see him, especially those who played with or against him, will tell you that he was a unique talent. Many of them still speak of him with wonder, including other wicketkeepers such as Len Maddocks, who kept for Australia in the mid-1950s. 'At his peak.' Maddocks says, 'Tallon was that far ahead of the rest of us it didn't matter.' Such people are not easily convinced that any keeper has reached the heights of performance behind the stumps that Tallon reached.

Tallon made this kind of impression on virtually all his contemporaries. To a man, it seems, they regard him as having been in a class of his own. This isn't merely a case of old players talking up someone of their own generation: it is true of players of the next generation, too, men like Alan Davidson who would naturally feel some allegiance to that other great Queensland keeper, Wally Grout, yet who unhesitatingly rate Tallon above all others. It is also true of the previous generation. Thus we find that, looking back, Don Bradman and Jack Fingleton, who played much of their Test cricket with Bert Oldfield, both named Tallon as the finest Australian keeper they had seen. So did three others from the Oldfield period, Bill O'Reilly, Hunter 'Stork' Hendry and Alan McGilvray, when consulted on the subject in the 1980s. The great leg-spinner Clarrie Grimmett went further. In a conversation in the late 1960s with the British playwright Ben Travers, Grimmett expressed the view that if he'd had Don Tallon instead of Oldfield behind the stumps throughout his Test career he would have taken twice as many wickets as he did.

The Tallon story is an interesting one, not least because it has never been told in full. The cricket writers of Tallon's day reported all he did on the field, of course, but they did not dwell on him as a character. Tallon's personality did not invite this. Somehow, he seemed too ordinary an individual to be turned into a celebrity, no matter how well he performed with the gloves. As a result, the Tallon story has not been writ as large in cricket history as it deserves to be. In particular, his contribution to the success and subsequent fame of Bradman's 1948 touring side in England has not been fully acknowledged. Tallon was not merely another member of a great team. Rather, being the best of wicketkeepers, he was one of the reasons the 1948 team was great.

Tallon was an immensely gifted individual, yet success did not come to him quickly or easily. In 1938, when he was 22, he looked to be on the verge of a long career as Australia's wicketkeeper. Australia was sending a team to England that year, and Tallon was a strong candidate. He would have been aware of this: he may well have pictured himself keeping wickets for Australia right through the 1940s and beyond. But things did not work out that way. In what Jack Pollard has called 'one of the most amazing blunders in the history of Australian cricket selection', Tallon was left out of the 1938 team. He performed superbly in the following domestic season, so superbly that nobody could doubt any longer that he was the finest keeper in the land. But before he could be considered again for Test selection war broke out, and Tallon had to wait another six years for a chance to play for Australia. Thus he had turned 30 by the time he played his first Test, and international cricket was to see him at his best for only a few years.

For much of his career Tallon had another problem to contend with: ill health. He developed stomach ulcers while still a young man, which were to afflict him, on and off, for the rest of his life. Given the seriousness of his condition, it is surprising he did not miss a lot more cricket than he did, and it is reasonable to assume that he often struggled through matches while suffering various degrees of discomfort or even illness. The only shortcoming people saw in Tallon's keeping while he was at his peak was an occasional lack of consistency: he sometimes had an off day when his sharpness and certainty seemed to desert him. People generally put this down to a lapse in concentration, but it is reasonable to speculate that the real explanation, more often than not, was that his ailment was distracting him. Anyone who has suffered from stomach ulcers would find this easy to understand. Tallon himself said that this had a lot to do with his slump in form in England in 1953, when he finally lost his place in the Australian side.

Bill Johnston, whose Test career roughly coincided with Tallon's, says that some of Tallon's catches and stumpings, including one or two off his own bowling, were so brilliant, so far beyond the ordinary scope of wicketkeeping, that bowlers found it hard to take credit for them. 'You'd recognise no other keeper in the world except Tallon could have done it, and you'd mentally put it down as a wicket you didn't altogether deserve,'

Johnston says. This is the theme of many of the assessments of Tallon that have been made by his contemporaries over the years: that his performance rose repeatedly to unmatched heights. It is what makes him such an interesting subject for study. Tallon was a talented golfer and a better-than-average snooker player, but he did not really excel at anything outside the cricket field. Moreover, by all accounts he possessed a casual, easy-going attitude to life, which you would not expect to find in a high achiever. How come, then, that in his area of specialty, wicketkeeping, he was quite possibly the best of all? It is a question, which anyone looking into the Tallon story must seek to answer.

2

THE BEGINNING

Research over the past 20 years, both in Australia and abroad, has reaffirmed the importance of practice in the development of sporting champions, especially in sports where skill is paramount. 'Practice' in this sense does not mean formal practice of the organised kind but, rather, any time spent playing a sport, even if only in the backyard. A recent study at Queensland University identified two other relevant factors. It was found that people who have a go at a variety of sports as children, both in the backyard and in formal competition, are much more likely to be champions than those who specialise early. It was also found that the sooner children compete with and against adults the better their chances are of making it to the top. Country children in Australia typically enjoy both advantages, which may explain why so many country-bred sports people have become champions.

The Tallon story fits the theory. He came from a large country town, Bundaberg; he played a number of sports as a boy, including cricket, rugby league, hockey and tennis; he played cricket against men from the age of twelve; and he played cricket endlessly in his backyard with his brothers right through his boyhood years. In his own words, he came 'from a family of cricket fanatics'. The Tallon family was well established in the Bundaberg area long before Don was born. Tallon's grandfather, Matthew Tallon, a Northern Ireland Presbyterian, arrived in Australia in 1869 and came to live in Bundaberg in 1881. By this time cricket had already taken root in Bundaberg. (The town's first club, the Burnett Cricket Club, was formed in 1876.) Matthew Tallon married, settled in North Bundaberg and worked as an engine driver on the railway, achieving the local distinction of being the first to drive a train on the Bundaberg-Mount Perry line. Later he worked as a toll collector on the Burnett River bridge. He died in 1920.

Don's father, Les Tallon, was born in 1888 and lived most of his childhood and adult life in North Bundaberg. He was a boilermaker by trade and worked at the Bundaberg Foundry, although during the Depression he was often unemployed and had to make do with whatever work he could find. At one time he worked as a curator at one of the cricket grounds in Bundaberg, a job for which he would have been well qualified, having long been an active player and umpire. As far back as the 1909-10 season, Les Tallon was one of the leading bowlers in the local competition, taking 44 wickets at 10.81 with his slow, accurate spin. He had four sons – Norm, Bill, Don and Matt – and two daughters, Doris and Jessie. Another child, a cousin of the Tallons, lived with them, so altogether there were nine mouths to feed in the Tallon household. Money, as might be expected, was often in short supply.

Don was born at Lady Chelmsford Hospital in Bundaberg on 17 February 1916. From the outset his health was delicate, and it is said that his mother, Catherine, had him photographed as a small boy to make sure she had something to remember him by in case he did not live. His distinguishing feature at this time was a mass of curly hair, which was widely admired and was a source of pride for his mother. His hair remained his best physical attribute: his sister Jessie remembers it as 'beautiful lady's hair.' In later years the hair was a source of some pride for Don himself, even if it did take some managing. In his younger days he used to wear a hat around the house before going out, hoping this would compress it and prevent the 'fuzzy-wuzzy' look which he liked to avoid.

Les Tallon's passion for cricket helped create an environment in which Don and his brothers were able to flourish as players: he was certainly the dominant influence in Don's early development in cricket. Tom Theodore, who grew up in Bundaberg about the same time, says that Les made a wicket for his sons in the backyard and insisted they practise there. Les was a strong-minded character, and to boys like Theodore he seemed a severe, authoritarian figure. 'He was the boss.' recalls Theodore. 'What he said you did.' Les Tallon knew enough about cricket to realise that in Don, and to a lesser extent Bill, he had sons blessed with exceptional talent for the game, and he pushed them to make the most of it. When Don looked certain to be picked for a rugby league representative team, Les contacted a local league official he knew and told him Don was not available. He wanted Don to concentrate on cricket. Don was not aware of this at the time and could not understand why he had not been picked. He did not find out until almost twenty years later when the league official told him about his father's intervention. The matter must have irked Tallon, for he sometimes spoke about it in later life, expressing regret at not having made the rugby league team after all.

The Tallons' backyard in Donald Street, North Bundaberg, proved an unusually successful cricket nursery. Three of the boys who played there went on to represent Queensland – Don, his old brother Bill and a boy about a year younger than Don named Jack McCarthy, who lived nearby. Don's childhood was typical of a country-town boy in the 1920s. He is remembered for his daring in pulling hairs out of horses' tails to make bird snares, a dangerous practice, which the headmaster at his school ordered him to discontinue. He loved playing marbles, probably because he was good at it, and made a point of going to school early each morning to get in a few games before classes started. Jack McCarthy's mother once called on Mrs Tallon to complain that Don had won a particularly valuable marble from her son.

There were two incidents in Tallon's boyhood years in Bundaberg which were to be lasting memories for him. One was the arrival of the Bundaberg aviator Bert Hinkler after a flight from Britain. 'I helped to push his plane down a bumpy road to his mother's place,' Tallon would recall. The other was the occasion he took up wicketkeeping. The story, as told by Tallon, was that the regular keeper for the North Bundaberg state school team failed to turn up and Don took his place. He bagged seven dismissals and kept the gloves thereafter. 'Wicketkeeping became a way of life for me,' he said. 'I was always juggling something in my hands – balls, oranges, lumps or rock.' By a fortunate coincidence, a capable wicketkeeper named Tom O'Shea, the son of the school's headmaster, Bill O'Shea, happened to be a student-teacher at the school and took young Tallon under his wing. He would later be credited with being the first person to instruct Tallon in the art of keeping.

Tallon could have been no older than eight when he took up keeping, for Tom Theodore, who often played against him in inter-school matches, is sure he was the North Bundaberg state school's keeper as far back as 1924. From the first, it seems, he performed behind the stumps with natural brilliance, and it was not long before he and his brother Bill, who bowled leg-breaks for the school, were the dominant players in Bundaberg's interschool cricket. 'Between the two of them they were a deadly combination,' recalls Theodore, who played for the South Bundaberg school.

Donny (as he was known to friends and family) was not only extravagantly talented but knew the tricks of the trade. One of young Tallon's ruses, according to a story handed down in Bundaberg, was to brush off the leg bail with the top of his pad if a ball passed close to the leg stump and then claim the batsman had been bowled. Indeed, the Tallons as a whole had a reputation for playing the game hard. Colin Stibe, another Bundaberg-raised cricketer of that period who went on to play for Queensland, was once given out for handling the ball in a club match in Bundaberg after he played the ball at his feet, picked it up and threw it back to the bowler, Les Tallon, who immediately appealed. Colin's brother, Percy Stibe, says Colin never forgot the incident. 'We played the game hard, too, after that,' he says.

Tallon's precocious talent did not take long to be noticed. As far back as the 1920s Australian cricket had an efficient system for bringing young players of potential to the fore, and young Tallon's reputation soon spread beyond Bundaberg. At thirteen he was chosen to captain Queensland schoolboys against New South Wales. A newspaper reporter covering the match, who wrote under the name Compo, singled out Tallon for praise. Compo wrote: 'Tallon (Bundaberg), the Queensland keeper, is recognised as the finest schoolboy wicketkeeper seen for many years. This boy captained the Queensland side well, this only being overshadowed by his polished work behind the stumps, the stumping of two batsmen being a revelation to many cricketers. This boy has a clean pair of hands and is very calm.'

Like many working-class boys of his generation, Tallon joined the work force after finishing primary school. He became an apprentice moulder at the Bundaberg Foundry where his father worked, although he left there a short time later and did odd jobs. His head was already full of cricket, it seems. By now, he had made a name for himself on the local cricket scene and was beginning to enjoy a degree of fame. After he made a bright 98 for Bundaberg's B side against Invicta, a nearby district side, the people who were there acclaimed him with extraordinary enthusiasm. A local newspaper reported: 'Donny was carried from the field, and held shoulder-high, while the cameras clicked. It was a wonderful display of batting for a boy.'

Even before leaving school Tallon had begun playing in the men's competition in Bundaberg. A photo thought to have been taken about 1930 shows the two Tallons, father and son, in a Bundaberg team playing in Rockhampton, and Don is wearing wicketkeeping gloves. By the end of the 1930-31 season, when the Sydney-based Test batsman Alan Kippax brought a team to Bundaberg, Tallon had been installed as keeper for Bundaberg's town team.

Kippax brought two teams to Bundaberg, the first of them in April 1927. Apart from Kippax himself, the side contained only a handful of prominent players, most notably Jack Gregory and Archie Jackson, both of whose wickets Les Tallon claimed. The second Kippax team, which came to Bundaberg in April 1931, was a more star-studded combination. As well as Kippax and Jackson, the side included Stan McCabe, Keith Rigg, O Wendell Bill, Alan Fairfax, Harold Hooker and the old-time New South Wales wicketkeeper Edgar 'Gar' Waddy. Don Bradman had been in the team, too, but a few days earlier, during a match at Rockhampton, he twisted his ankle. When the two-day match against Bundaberg began at the Recreation Reserve in Bundaberg's West End, Bradman was still laid up in a Rockhampton hospital.

Although Tallon had kept occasionally for Bundaberg, the side's regular keeper was a player named Bob Morrison. Young as he was, Tallon was preferred for the important match against Kippax's team, and it is Percy Stibe's recollection that this was when Tallon became

Bundaberg's regular keeper. He performed modestly enough, claiming no dismissals and scoring just 5 not out, yet Kippax is said to have named him later as one of the two most promising players he saw on the entire tour. The journalist Jim Holledge told a story about this match which he apparently obtained from Tallon himself. Archie Jackson was batting when Bundaberg's left-arm wrist spinner Jack Pizzey, later to become Premier of Queensland, came on to bowl, and at first Jackson seemed uncertain against him. Jackson turned to Tallon behind the stumps and asked him about Pizzey's bowling. The boy Tallon, happy to be consulted by so famous a batsman, volunteered the information that Pizzey could not bowl a wrong'un. This was all Jackson needed to know, and he proceeded to play Pizzey with ease. Poor Pizzey took a hammering and ended the innings with 2 for 144.

This match gave Tallon his first brush with the game's famous. In a sense, it was also his coming of age as a cricketer. From now on, the big advances in his cricket career would be made not in Bundaberg but in the wider cricket world beyond.

3
A Move Up

The year Don Tallon turned 16 was an eventful one for Australian cricket. It was the year England's bowlers directed their bodyline attack against Australia's batsmen, creating a controversy that was to shake the cricket world to its foundations. The bodyline summer, 1932-33, was an eventful one for Tallon, too. By now, word had got around in cricket circles in Brisbane that an exceptionally talented young wicketkeeper-batsman had emerged in Bundaberg. In the previous season, when he played in Brisbane during Country Week, Tallon had come under the spotlight in a most unusual way. Our knowledge of this comes from of all places the Melbourne Argus, which in November 1933 published an article by a journalist named Owen O'Brien, who had worked in Bundaberg and obviously knew all about young Tallon. He reported that two years earlier, when 15-year-old Tallon played in Country Week, he made such an impression that Queensland's Shield selectors arranged a private trial for him at the Gabba, during which he kept to bowlers in the Queensland side, including Eddie Gilbert. O'Brien said Tallon 'gave a brilliant display' and so impressed the selectors with his sureness, speed and finish that they decided his future had to be protected. Accordingly, O'Brien said, they asked the Bundaberg Cricket Association to take the gloves away from Tallon for a season to allow his hands to mature.

Whether or not this request was received in Bundaberg, it does not seem Tallon gave up the gloves. In 1931-32 he and Jack Pizzey played for North Country against South Country in Brisbane at Graceville. Perhaps it was then that Tallon attracted the attention of a prominent Toombul club official named Norm Plaisted, who invited him to move to Brisbane and join the Toombul club for the 1932-33 season. Plaisted made the transfer to Brisbane possible by providing him with a job in his sawmill and Tallon found a home with cousins in Brisbane. He was so homesick at first that he used to go to the Roma Street Railway Station when the train from Bundaberg was due to arrive in the hope of meeting someone he knew.

In early February 1933, when Tallon was not quite 17 years old, he had his first taste of international cricket: he played for Queensland Country against the touring England side at Toowoomba. The match was played against a background of controversy over the Englishmen's bowling, which had come to a head in the third Test at Adelaide a fortnight earlier.

Harold Larwood, the spearhead of the bodyline attack, played at Toowoomba and bowled Tallon for 2. Tallon did have one notable success with the gloves. He stumped the England batsman Herbert Sutcliffe for 19. The Toowoomba Chronicle said Sutcliffe had reached forward to play the veteran leg-spinner Hunter Poon. It must have been a smart piece of work, for the newspaper commented: 'Young Tallon (wicketkeeper) gave a fine exhibition and his stumping of Sutcliffe was a masterpiece.' He was reliable, too. In England's innings of 376 he conceded only five byes.

Tallon's job at the sawmill lasted until the end of the cricket season. After that, he went home to Bundaberg, did some odd jobs and kept fit in the winter playing hockey. A 1933 photo shows him as a member of the pennant-winning Burnett Hockey Club side. He also kept fit skipping, his favourite exercise. Tallon believed it kept him light on his feet. He was back in Brisbane for the following cricket season, 1933-34, although he was now playing for another club, Colts.

The season had barely begun when Tallon received a startling promotion: he was picked to play for Queensland in a Sheffield Shield match against Victoria in Brisbane. He was not a stand-in replacement, either. The incumbent Queensland keeper, Harry Leeson, was available, but Tallon was chosen ahead of him. Tallon was 17 years, nine months and 14 days old. From this distance it is impossible to say what motivated the selectors to pick someone so young, but we may assume they decided he was a player of such rare potential that they could afford to overlook his lack of experience. One selector in particular had a high opinion of Tallon's ability – Jack Holdsworth, a Queensland selector from 1923-24 until 1941-42, who may well have organised the trial at the Gabba two years earlier. He was later given the credit for being the first to recognise Tallon's potential.

Tallon had come a long way in a short time. Only a couple of years earlier it had been a big step-up for him to keep wickets for Bundaberg. Now, suddenly, he was one of the game's national elite and rubbing shoulders with players he must have grown up revering – men of like Bill Ponsford and Bill Woodfull, both of whom played in this match. It was not a happy game for Tallon. Queensland lost by an innings, and Tallon's own contribution was minimal. He made 17 and 3 and figured in just one dismissal behind the stumps, catching Ponsford off Ron Oxenham's bowling for 55. Earlier, he missed an easy stumping when Keith Rigg was well out of his ground, but the catch he took to dismiss Ponsford was reported to have been performed 'in a flash' and to have been greeted with general applause. Tallon was still boy-sized when he made the Queensland team. He did not shoot up to his adult height (5 feet 11 inches or 180cm, according to his passport) until a year or so later.

Tallon's debut match for Queensland was played at the Gabba from 1 to 5 December 1933. The Queensland team left for its annual southern tour a few days later, but Tallon was not included. Perhaps the selectors felt it would all be too much for him. Instead, he travelled to Sydney with Queensland's colts team in late December for the annual match against NSW colts. Tallon had played in the same match a season earlier in Brisbane and, apart from stumping a promising Sydney all-rounder named Ginty Lush, who was to play many matches for NSW both before and after the war, he did nothing to attract special attention. In this Sydney match, though, he made a bigger impression . He scored 69 not out, the side's second-highest score, against a bowling line-up which included the future Test bowler Ernie Toshack, and the Queenslanders won the match.

He also stumped Lush again. A photo in Sydney Morning Herald captured the moment: Lush has swung at and missed a ball outside the leg stump, apparently dragging over the line as he did so, and Tallon has whipped off the bails. It must have all happened in an instant, for although the bails are still in the air Lush has moved his toe back over the line. Tallon's batting earned a mention in the newspaper's report of the match, which noted that he had shown 'a desire to attack the bowling.' There were other admirers. Ernie Hutcheon, who wrote a history of Queensland cricket in the 1930s, said Tallon impressed NSW observers both with his batting and his keeping.

Tallon was clearly a talent worth nurturing. Queensland cricket authorities found work for him as a groundsman's assistant at the Gabba, one of his jobs being to erect and dismantle the practice nets. The work was hardly demanding. According to Tallon, he spent as much time practising in the Gabba nets with two other Queensland cricketers employed there, the Aboriginal fast bowler Eddie Gilbert and Tommy Allen, as he did working. Gilbert was 10 years older than Tallon, but the two got on well. Gilbert once stayed with the Tallons on a visit to Bundaberg, and long afterwards, in 1966, Tallon went to visit him when he was patient at the big mental hospital at Goodna near Brisbane.

Tallon returned to the Queensland side for the last match of the 1933-34 season, against South Australia at the Gabba. For Tallon, the most significant moment of this match was his stumping of Bert Tobin off the bowling of Oxenham, the first of his 129 stumpings in first-class cricket.

Having played in this match, Tallon must have begun the next season, 1934-35, full of hope, yet he was overlooked for Queensland's first fixture, against South Australia in Brisbane. The state selectors then sprang another surprise: although they picked Harry Leeson as keeper for the southern tour starting a few days later they also picked Tallon, the idea being that Tallon would play as a batsman. This is what happened in the first two matches of the tour, against Victoria and South Australia, but for the final tour match against NSW in Sydney Tallon took over the gloves and Leeson was made 12th man. It was a landmark event in Tallon's career, for it marked the beginning of his permanent tenure of Queensland's wicketkeeping position. He was to wear the gloves for Queensland whenever he was available to play for almost 20 years.

Tallon was 18 years old when he went on that first southern tour. According to stories handed down within the Tallon family, he felt nervous about it beforehand. He was a shy, rather introverted country youth and, according to his sister Jessie, who heard it from her mother, the prospect of 'mixing with different society' alarmed him. Where his cricket was concerned, though, he seemed to have no self-doubts: Tallon always knew how talented he was. The fact that he was chosen solely as a batsman for two Shield matches at the age of 18 shows the direction in which others saw his talent heading. Indeed, in his first few years of big cricket Tallon was generally looked upon as a batsman-wicketkeeper as much as a wicketkeeper-batsman, which is why more than commentator in later years, including Bill O'Reilly, would bemoan the fact that Tallon did not come close to realising his early batting potential.

Even at this early stage of Tallon's career he had begun to attract admirers. One Sunday he played in a match at Perry Park in Brisbane and was watched by a seven-year-old boy named Wally Grout, who recalled the occasion in his book My Country's Keeper. If Grout was correct about his age, this would have been the summer of 1934-35. Grout was supposed to be home by 1 pm to attend Sunday school, but he became 'so engrossed in the match and the magic of Tallon' that he lost track of the time and received a beating with a strap when he arrived home late.

Match by match, over the next few seasons, Tallon began to make his mark at the national level. In 1935-36, against an MCC side which included a few English players of note including Joe Hardstaff, Tallon claimed six dismissals in one innings, five of them stumpings and four of these off the leg-break bowling of his Gabba workmate Tommy Allen. In his very next match, against Victoria, he claimed four dismissals in an innings, three of them stumpings. His batting was flourishing, too. In February 1936, a couple of weeks before he turned 20, Tallon played a magnificent innings of 193 against Victoria at the Gabba, scoring at better than a run a minute (he was at the crease for 187 minutes) and hitting one six and 28 fours. In this same match, he claimed five dismissals in an innings. In Brisbane grade cricket, too, he had run hot with the bat, topping the averages in 1935-36 averages with 343 runs at 57.16.

Tallon was clearly a player on the rise, and his name was now being mentioned in high places. Hence his selection to play in a testimonial match staged in Sydney on behalf of two greats of the past, Warren Bardsley and Jack Gregory, at the beginning of the 1936-37 season. The match amounted to a trial for national selection. One side, led by Vic Richardson, was chosen from Australian players who had toured South Africa the previous summer, while the other, led by Don Bradman, was made up of other players likely to press for a place in the coming Test series. Tallon was one of these. He played for Bradman's XI and batted at number five in the order.

Tallon failed with the bat in this game, but in his first Shield match of the season a few weeks later, against NSW at the Gabba, he scored 100 in strange circumstances. Tallon was out for 96, caught behind by Bert Oldfield, who then notified the umpire that Tallon had previously got some bat to a ball which had been counted as four byes. As a result, the umpire instructed the scorer to amend the scoresheet accordingly, which meant Tallon was credited with a century. It was a thoughtful gesture by Oldfield, who is known to have admired the youngster's keeping, although some suspected Oldfield was also influenced by a desire to maintain a byeless record for the match. In fact, the four runs having been credited to Tallon, the scorebook did not show a single bye against Oldfield's name in either Queensland innings.

Before the year was out Tallon had scored another Shield century, his third in four Shield matches – 101 against South Australia at Adelaide in late December. Then, against Victoria at the Gabba in mid-January, he almost scored another. He was bowled by Hans Ebeling for 96. Tallon was clearly one of the form batsmen in the country. He was a splendid driver, in particular, the cover drive being his pet shot, and he timed the ball sweetly enough to hit sixes when he was in the mood to do so. At this point in his career some would have predicted for him a future in Test cricket as a batsman. Nobody then could have imagined that so far as his batting was concerned this would be his heyday – that he would never again recapture the form he showed as 20-year-old in 1936-37.

4
THE SHOCK OF 1938

The sports historian Jack Pollard, a friend of the cricket writer Ray Robinson, says that in Robinson's later years, when he was reflecting on cricketers he had watched during half a century or more of reporting on the game, he would sometimes speak of Don Tallon's wicketkeeping in the last few seasons before World War II. It was Robinson's view that Tallon in his early 20s attained a degree of excellence unmatched by any other keeper he ever knew, before or since. The pity is the cricket world saw so little of Tallon then. The outbreak of war forced the cancellation of the Tests against England in 1940-41, when Tallon would probably have been an automatic choice, but nobody in cricket could be held responsible for that. His omission from the 1938 tour of England was another matter. Many people, especially in Queensland, felt it was an error for which the selectors should indeed be held responsible.

There had seemed three main contenders for the two wicketkeeping positions: the Victorian Ben Barnett, Tallon and the veteran Bert Oldfield, now 43 years old but still performing efficiently for NSW. Barnett and Tallon seemed the most likely pairing, but some thought Oldfield and Tallon, the old master and the rising star, would be the two chosen. In fact, neither made the team. The selectors chose Barnett and Charlie Walker of South Australia. Why? The question was to generate speculation for years to come. Tallon's admirers in Queensland saw his omission as so unfair, so contrary to reason, that they felt there had to be some hidden factor.

Various theories did the rounds. One was that the selectors were unimpressed by the fact Tallon stood back to Geoff Cook's medium pace. Tallon did stand back to Cook, but only when the ball was swinging. When the shine was gone, Tallon stood up. Another theory was that the selectors had doubts about Tallon's ability to keep to the Australian wrist spinners, especially Bill O'Reilly and Chuck Fleetwood-Smith. These doubts would have been unfounded, for Tallon kept superbly to wrist spinners. Indeed, it is reasonable to speculate that if Tallon had been chosen instead of Walker as the side's number-two keeper he would have taken over from Barnett as the Test keeper before the series ended. When Barnett failed to stump Len Hutton at 40 off Fleetwood-Smith's bowling in the final Test (one of the most costly of all misses, given that Hutton went on to score 364), many Queenslanders must thought to themselves that the miss would not have occurred if their Don had been behind the stumps.

In 1950 an unnamed writer in People magazine (he may well have been the cricketer-turned-journalist Dick Whitington) voiced a rumour which had been doing the rounds and continued to do the rounds for some time. This was that Tallon had been left out in 1938 because he did not possess the social graces to conduct himself properly in England. The rumour, the writer of the article said, was that Tallon was not 'classy' enough in his talk and ways to travel with an Australian team. Whether there was any truth in this nobody can now say, but it is at least worth noting that the same suggestion was made to explain the omission from the 1930 Ashes touring side of the spin bowler Bert Ironmonger, who, like Tallon, came from a provincial Queensland background.

Ray Robinson discussed the matter of Tallon's omission at length in his 1950 book From The Boundary. Robinson's own view was that the simple fact Tallon came from Queensland stood against him. 'I believe he would have been chosen had he been keeper for one of the older cricketing states,' Robinson said.

Robinson may have been right. There can be little doubt that then and for years afterwards Queenslanders found it harder than players from the southern states to make the Test side. It is difficult to believe, for instance, that Ken 'Slasher' Mackay would not have played for Australia a few years earlier than he did if he had come from Sydney or Melbourne instead of Brisbane. Asked why Tallon had been overlooked in 1938, a Queensland team-mate of many years, Ernie Toovey, said, simply: 'He was a Queenslander.' This was the Queensland view, and it may have been the correct one.

In fairness to the selectors, it should be noted that Tallon did not really turn in any attention-grabbing performances in the season preceding the 1938 tour: there were no multiple-wicket hauls of the kind that had caused a stir a season or two earlier which would have made it harder for the selectors to leave him out. Moreover, after his run glut of the previous year, he had a poor summer with the bat, his highest Shield score being 48. So Tallon stayed behind and Charlie Walker went. For many, this was a double surprise. As Bill O'Reilly observed later, Tallon's exclusion was 'a mystery commensurate with Walker's inclusion.' Four years later, however, after Walker was killed in action piloting a bomber over Germany, nobody would have begrudged him the satisfaction of having made that 1938 tour.

How did Tallon react to the disappointment? Typically, it seems he did not dwell on it for long. His brother Matt recalled many years later: 'He never bellyached. If anything, it made him determined to keep playing.' Yet the experience did leave a scar of a kind. Thereafter, even when his supremacy as a keeper was acknowledged by all, Tallon was said to be always fearful of being dropped and to suffer intense anxiety whenever the Australian side was to be chosen.

The players on the 1938 Ashes tour had barely returned when Tallon showed what he was capable of. In the opening Shield match of the 1938-39 season, played against NSW at the Gabba in late November, Tallon claimed six dismissals in one innings, three by stumpings, one of which was off the bowling of his brother Bill, who was playing his first first-class match. Against the same team a month later in Sydney, Tallon claimed six in each innings, thus equalling a 70–year–old world record for 12 dismissals in a match held by the Surrey keeper Edward Pooley. Tallon caught nine and stumped three.

In the following week, batting at the Gabba against South Australia, Tallon hit what the next day's paper described as a 'scintillating' century. He made 115 in 164 minutes, batting with 'reckless abandon', according to a newspaper report. This success with the bat, closely following as it did his wicketkeeping record, was for Queenslanders a confirmation of the injustice Tallon suffered by being left out of the Ashes touring side. A Brisbane newspaper commented: 'As a keeper-batsman, Don is certainly "Tallon" the world that his omission from the last Test team was a tragedy for Australian cricket.'

Tallon's fellow townsman Colin Stibe made his first-class debut in this match and scored 58. There were thus three Bundaberg-bred players in the Queensland side, Stibe and the Tallon brothers, while a fourth, Jack McCarthy, who had played one match for the state a few years earlier, was pressing for a place. Tallon injured his thumb in this match and his captain, Bill Brown, took over the gloves. Charles 'Chilla' Christ, a left-arm spinner, made a ball bounce sharply while Brown was keeping. It caught the edge of Jack Badcock's bat but came too suddenly for Brown to hold, although he did manage to deflect it to Rex Rogers at first slip, who took the catch. Later, Brown asked Tallon how on earth any wicketkeeper could be expected to cope with such a ball. 'You just watch it off the bat and catch it,' Tallon said in a matter-of-fact way. Brown never forgot that reply, for he felt it gave an insight into Tallon's skill.

Tallon was to produce one more memorable performance before the 1938-39 summer was over. Against Victoria at the Gabba in early February, he secured seven dismissals in an innings, four of them stumpings, thus equalling another world record. One of the stumpings was off the bowling of his brother Bill: the old North Bundaberg state school combination was still functioning well. Of the 21 wickets which Bill Tallon took in a short first-class career spanning the 1938-39 and 1939-40 seasons, five were stumpings by his brother.

In grade cricket in 1938-39, Don Tallon indulged his fondness for bowling leg-breaks. Having changed clubs again before the season began, moving from Colts to Souths, he bowled 81.5 overs and took 20 wickets at 17.60, the ninth best average in the competition. Errold La Frantz, who made the Queensland side just before the war, played for Toombul against Tallon in a grade match in 1939-40, in which Tallon was responsible for all nine dismissals (Toombul batted a man short). Tallon caught the first four, then gave the gloves to someone else and took the other five wickets with his leg spin. 'I don't know of this happening previously here in Queensland,' La Frantz says. 'It certainly has not occurred since.'

Tallon's feats in Sheffield Shield cricket in 1938-39 could have left few in doubt about his supremacy among Australian keepers. He not only equalled two world records but finished the Shield season with an outstanding overall result: six matches, 34 dismissals, 21 catches, 13 stumpings. He was now a player in demand. A few days after he equalled the record for dismissals in an innings, he was reported to have received two private offers to move to Sydney. To prevent him going, a job was arranged for him at the Brisbane motor company Eagers. His hopes must now have been fixed on the coming Test series in 1940-41 against the Englishmen. But those hopes, like the hopes of countless others, were to be dashed by the outbreak of war.

5
THE MAN AT WORK

Bill Brown, who knew both Bert Oldfield and Don Tallon well as keepers, had this to say when asked to compare them: 'Oldfield was one of the most efficient wicketkeepers I've ever seen. He was always in position, he had beautiful hands. What he lacked was the speed and – what should I call it? – the imagination of Tallon. They were on a par technically – in fact, technically Oldfield was possibly better – but Tallon was dynamic. He would make things happen. The game would be going along and all of a sudden he'd take a catch on the legside or stump some fella on the legside and transform the match.'

The streak of brilliance in Tallon's keeping was a cause of occasional wonder for everyone who played with him. As Godfrey Evans, his opposite number in the England team, described it, Tallon's reflexes enabled him to make 'the most improbable dismissals look outrageously straightforward.' Yet Tallon's brilliance was really no more than the gloss on a sound technique. He was, above all, a safe, technically correct, highly reliable keeper. Don Bradman, who studied both Oldfield and Tallon closely, thought Tallon's keeping 'abnormally safe'. Bradman cited two reasons for rating him above Oldfield. One was that Tallon covered more ground on the legside when keeping to fast bowlers. The other, significantly, was that he made fewer mistakes.

For anyone wishing to analyse Tallon's keeping, this has to be the starting point. At his top, Tallon missed very few chances. Indeed, when age eventually took its toll and he began to lose his touch, the difference everyone noticed was not a loss of brilliance, for he continued to perform dazzling feats until the end, but the appearance of errors.

What was the essence of his skill? Cricketers who studied Tallon's methods at first hand formed different views about this. Stan Sismey, who kept for NSW before and after the war, concluded that Tallon's powers of anticipation were the key. 'He was always very smooth, very efficient, very confident of his own ability,' Sismey said, 'but his anticipation was the main thing. Particularly with the fast bowlers. Tallon would make extra catches for them, not just accept the ones than came along.' Sismey once caught a batsman off a leg glance in a Shield match in Sydney. He ended up sprawled on the grass with the ball in his outstretched left glove and was congratulated by nearby fieldsmen – although not by his captain, Keith Miller, who was fielding at first slip. According to Sismey, Miller looked at him and said, 'Sisso, Don Tallon would have caught that in his right hand standing up,' a remark which brought Sismey back to earth.

Tallon was tallish, lithe, rangy and fluent in all his movements. (He was even a good dancer.) His instinct for moving in advance of the ball was clearly one of the hallmarks of his keeping and explains his most memorable catches. There are many testimonies to it. Here is one from Alan Davidson, who toured New Zealand with Tallon in 1949-50 with a second-string Australian side: 'I bowled one to Merv Wallace which started on the off stump and moved to leg. Wallace played a legitimate leg-glance – and Tallon caught it between his thighs. He must have been four or five yards to the legside. Whereas other blokes might have dived and got a glove to it, here was Tallon actually waiting for it.'

Tallon was available to go on that New Zealand tour in 1949-50 because he had pulled out of the Australian tour of South Africa the same summer. His place in the Australian side was taken by Ron Saggers, a polished performer from NSW, who had as his deputy the efficient South Australian Gil Langley. Both were keepers of the highest class, yet to other members of the Australian team, who were accustomed to Tallon's flair, the difference was striking. One of them says that for the first half of the tour, whenever a South African batsman played a leg glance, he would automatically raise his arms in expectation of a catch, a habit he developed while playing with Tallon.

Wally Grout was 19 years old and already regarded as Queensland's number-two keeper when Tallon played in the first Test of the 1946-47 series at the Gabba. Grout watched the match and made a point of studying Tallon's technique. 'Watching him closely I felt I could match his work on the off but never had I seen such leg-side coverage,' Grout wrote in his autobiography. 'Here was my model. I noted how he never snatched at the ball but let it ride gently into his gloves. And I began to adopt his practice of trying to take the ball on the legside with my right glove so that the left was free to stretch for a thick edge.'

The practice of moving far enough to take balls outside the leg stump in the right glove and those outside the off in the left came to regarded as one of the trademarks of Tallon's keeping. Tallon explained the logic of it in an interview in 1968. 'I liked to try to play outside the break,' he said. 'Most snicks come off the outside edge. If I took the ball in my right hand on the leg side, I still had my left hand outside the line if there was a snick. Similarly, you moved far to the right for a leg-spinner bowling outside the off stump.'

Keepers around the world have since adopted, or tried to adopt, the same method. Did Tallon originate it? Len Maddocks, whose first-class career began in 1946-47, says it was certainly his understanding then as a young keeper that it was a Tallon innovation. 'My belief then was that he was the first to do it, and my guess is he was the first with footwork fast enough to allow him to do it,' Maddocks said. In Maddocks' opinion, footwork was the basis of Tallon's skill. As a young keeper he would go to the MCG whenever Tallon was playing there in a Test and glue his eyes on Tallon's feet. 'He had everything,' Maddocks said. 'He was a tall bloke for a keeper, but he had better footwork than anyone I've ever seen. He had magic gloves. Gil Langley and I were competing with each other, if you like. Gil had crook footwork but tremendous hands. Tallon had both: tremendous footwork and tremendous hands.'

Godfrey Evans, too, seemed to think Tallon invented the technique of covering for the unexpected edged catch. This is what he wrote on the subject: 'I used to watch closely the technique of Don Tallon, my opposite number in the Australian Test series in 1948. I regard him as the greatest of wicketkeepers. He had such grace and ease of movement, and he always took the ball so cleanly, always in the right position, never off balance. One of the things which I tried to copy from him was the way in which he moved far enough over to enable him to take leg-side balls to the right of his body and more in the right hand than the left. This gave him greater freedom of movement and better sight of the ball. And when the batsman did get a touch on the leg side, or even played a genuine leg glance, Tallon was half-way there already for the catch. Watching him helped me to take Alec Bedser's in-swingers and to be ready for a leg-side catch or stumping.'

The catches Tallon took wide on the legside were one of two features of his keeping which people marvelled at. The other was his stumping, invariably performed, as Ray Robinson once described it, with camera-shutter speed. His stumping was so fast, so sudden, that it defied attempts by team-mates to work out quite how he did it. Bill Brown came to this conclusion: 'When Tallon stumped, the stumping started before the ball got to him. He didn't take the ball and then go looking for the stumps. He performed a sort of sweeping movement, taking the ball on the way and then on to the stumps.' This all happened with a speed which beat the eye. 'Lightning' was the word people often used. Bradman said Tallon was 'like lightning in his stumpings'. Bill O'Reilly wrote: 'I have never seen a keeper to compare with Tallon when he went through his stumping routine. He was lightning fast.' When Peter Burge made the Queensland team in the 1950s he heard from older players that Tallon's legside stumpings off the medium-pacer Geoff Cook, just before and after the war, were so fast that the scorers sometimes had to ask the umpires at the next interval whether the batsman had been stumped or bowled.

Speed was not all that set him apart. Whether deliberately or not, Tallon made a practice when stumping of causing minimal disturbance to the stumps. Often he removed only a single bail. Alan Davidson tells this story about an incident on the 1949-50 tour of New Zealand: 'Jack Iverson bowled a ball down the leg side which turned even further away. Tallon took the ball out wide, whipped it towards the bails and appealed for a stumping. The umpire at square leg turned down the appeal, saying, "You haven't taken the bails off." Tallon held up his glove and said, "What's this?". The ball was in the centre of the glove and there, held between the thumb and forefinger, was the bail. He'd picked up the bail as he swept his glove past the stumps, but he did it too fast for the umpire to see. Because the stumps were undisturbed and there was no bail lying on the ground, the umpire assumed the bail were intact.' Davidson adds: "I saw him do a lot of stumpings, but they never had to rearrange the stumps afterwards, no matter where he stumped from. He was just so far above any other keeper I've ever seen. I never saw anyone who was even close to him. It was as if he had inbuilt radar. Most keepers grab at the ball momentarily before they stump. Tallon had this amazing timing: his hands were always moving forwards to stump as he took the ball.'

Timing is the key to taking the ball sweetly, and keepers who do take it sweetly are said to have 'soft hands'. Ken Archer, who played with Tallon in both the Queensland and Test sides, has a special memory of Tallon's soft hands. Like other young players with a strong throw, Archer liked to return the ball hard from the covers, where he often fielded, and hear it crash into the keeper's gloves. When Tallon was the keeper, he says, he never had this satisfaction, for Tallon took the ball almost noiselessly, a sign of near-perfect timing. Archer says that in his experience Tallon was unique in this respect. When he threw hard to Grout, for instance, he would always hear the ball bang into the gloves. 'Don never made a sound,' Archer says. 'He didn't have an exaggerated recoil like some keepers do. He just had this beautiful reflex timing . . . the softest, loveliest hands.'

A competitive spirit sharpened Tallon's physical talents. The English commentator John Arlott had this mind when he wrote of him: 'The surname tells everything – instinctively prehensile, naturally predatory.' It was a common observation by batsmen who played against Tallon that he exuded a sense of menace. He did not harass them, of course, for that would not have been acceptable at the time. On the contrary: he had a habit of greeting each new batsman with a smile. The England batsman Denis Compton thought it was a 'good luck' smile. Tallon's reputation alone was enough to make batsmen feel uneasy, for they knew any slip was death.

Although he was almost taciturn by nature, Tallon was a noisy, aggressive appealer, especially when he was still making his way up the cricket ladder. Australian batsmen were by and large accustomed to this and prepared to tolerate it, but some English players resented it when they encountered it for the first time in 1946-47. Clif Cary, who wrote a book about that series, cited Tallon's 'impetuous' appealing as the one flaw in his game, noting that he had been accused of making more appeals in two Tests than Bert Oldfield or the former England keeper Herbert Strudwick made in a whole series. Tallon toned down his appealing in later years, but the notoriety lived with him. When he came out to bat in Don Bradman's testimonial match in Melbourne in December 1948, the fielding side played a joke on him. On the first occasion Tallon played and missed, every fieldsman appealed, even though his bat was nowhere near the ball.

Among some opponents Tallon also had a reputation for gamesmanship. Godfrey Evans wrote of him: 'It used to be said that he would get you out by fair means or foul,' from which we may deduce that one or more England batsmen thought Tallon had secured their dismissal with some kind of sharp practice. Tallon certainly did not abide by the gentleman's code of appealing only when he thought the batsman was out – as Len Maddocks once discovered to his cost.

Maddocks' first played against Tallon in a Shield match at the MCG in December 1947. Maddocks was then 21 years old, and this was his fourth first-class match. After scoring 20, he found himself facing Mick Raymer, a left-arm orthodox spinner. Tallon was behind the stumps. "He bowled a ball just outside my legs, which I tried to leg-glance,' Maddocks says, 'but I missed it and it hit my pads. Tallon took it and appealed and the umpire gave me out. I didn't drink in those days, and at the end of the day's play I was having a glass of lemonade and listening to the older players talking. Tallon came into our dressing room and said, "Did you learn anything today, son?" I didn't know what he was talking about. Tallon said to me: "Always appeal and leave it to the umpire – that's his job." He knew he'd caught me off my pads – probably no one else did, but he and I did – and he was just making the point to me, a kid coming into the game, that in a close decision it was the umpire's job to say in or out.'

Did Tallon have a weakness as a keeper? On his good days, apparently not – and most of his days were good days. His weakness was that he did have an occasional off day, even while he was still at his peak immediately after the war. Opponents like Denis Compton were puzzled by this. In a book he wrote after the 1946-47 Ashes series, Compton said: 'One day he would snap everything up. The next, chances would be missed. We noticed this in the Tests.' Compton called Tallon a 'wicketkeeper extraordinary, the man who frequently makes superb catches off chances that no do not by rights exist and, a day later, is nothing like the artist we had all admired so much.' Andy Flanagan, who wrote a book about the 1948 Ashes series, noticed the same thing. 'On his day he reaches dizzy heights with his keeping,' he said, 'but due to weak opposition in many county games he suffered occasional lapses from lack of concentration.'

But was a lack of concentration really to blame? One of Tallon's contemporaries, when asked to explain Tallon's off days, said: 'It's pretty hard to keep well when you're suffering from a hangover.' He was suggesting Tallon kept badly when he drank heavily the night before. Tallon enjoyed a drink – this was widely known in the cricket fraternity – but other team-mates insist his drinking did not affect his cricket during his playing days. A long-time Queensland team-mate said: 'I can honestly say I never saw him under the influence all the time I was playing with him.' According to an Australian team-mate, Tallon reputation for drinking owed much to the fact that he was easily affected by alcohol. 'In his playing days Donny actually didn't drink all that much – I know that because I used to drink with him myself,' he says. 'I know a lot of other guys who drank a lot more than he did and yet were regarded as sober, temperate members of the team.' The other possibility, raised in an earlier chapter, is that Tallon often took the field while suffering from the stomach ulcers and associated ailments that were to afflict him from his mid-twenties. From this time onwards, in fact, illness was to be a backdrop to everything Tallon did, on and off the field.

Young Tallon with the curls which were his
mother's pride © 1

Tallon in his first pair of long whites on a
trip to Rockhampton with the Bundaberg
team about 1930. He is pictured here with
his team's manager Les Frawley, a
prominant Bundaberg cricket official © 2

The Tallons, father and son, in the Bundagerg team which played at Rockhampton
about 1930. Young Tallon, then aged about 14, is wearing the gloves and his father, Les
on the far left in the front row. Tom Theodore is third from the left in the back row. © 3

Seventeen-year-old Tallon stumps Ginty Lush in the NSW – Queensland Colts match in Sydney, December, 1933. © 4

Tallon uses his feet against the South Australian spinner Frank Ward at Adelaide in January 1939. Tallon made 115 in this innings. The wicketkeeper is Charlie Walker, chosen ahead of Tallon on the previous year's tour of England. He was killed on a bombing raid over Germany four years later. © 5

The young keeper. The former England Wicketkeeper George Duckworth said of Tallon: 'He gets smoothly to balls that would have me scrambling. In fielding the balls with gloves on he is the cleanest I have ever seen.' © 6

DON TALLON

A studio portrait of Tallon in the mid–1930s © 7

At Sydney in January 1937 this Queensland Side beat NSW (admittedly weakened by the absence of its Test players) for the first time in 10 years. Tallon is second from the left in the front row. (Back row) (from left) – D Hansen, G Amos, L Dixon, E Wyeth, G Gunthorpe, G Cook, G Baker: (Front row) – W Andrews, D Tallon, R Oxenham (Captain), T Williams (manager) T Allen, R Rodgers. © 8

Tallon and his boyhood friend Jack McCarthy during their visit to Sydney in December 1940 as members of the Queensland team. © 9

The master stumper at practice. His Australian team-mate Neil Harvey says: 'I would say he was the quickest stumper I've ever seen . He never made a mess of the stumps. Often you'd see just one bail go – clunk! He was so quick. In those days he has some good slow bowlers to keep to. I've seen blokes just run over the line and in a flash one bail would be off. He was so elegant, too – nothing rough or untidy about what he did. He was the complete keeper.' © 10

Tallon (far left) with Queensland team–mates in Sydney in December 1940. © 11

Tallon and two fellow soldiers. © 12

Tallon's first tour with an Australian team was to New Zealand in March 1946. Here, the team is at Wellington: back row (from left) – W Watts, Don Tallon, Keith Miller, Bill O'Reilly, Ernie Toshack, Bruce Dooland, Ron Hamence, E C Yeomans (manager): Front row (from left) – Ian Johnson, Colin McCool, Lindsay Hassett, Bill Brown (captain), Sid Barnes, Ken Meuleman, Ray Lindwall. © 13

The Australian team which met England at Brisbane in the post-war Ashes Test in 1946. Back row (front left) – Keith Miller, Ernie Toshack, Don Tallon: Middle row (from left) – Ian Johnson, Arthur Morris, Ray Lindwall, Colin McCool: Front row (from left) – Ken Meuleman, Lindsay Hassett, Don Bradman (captain), Sid Barnes, George Tribe. © 14

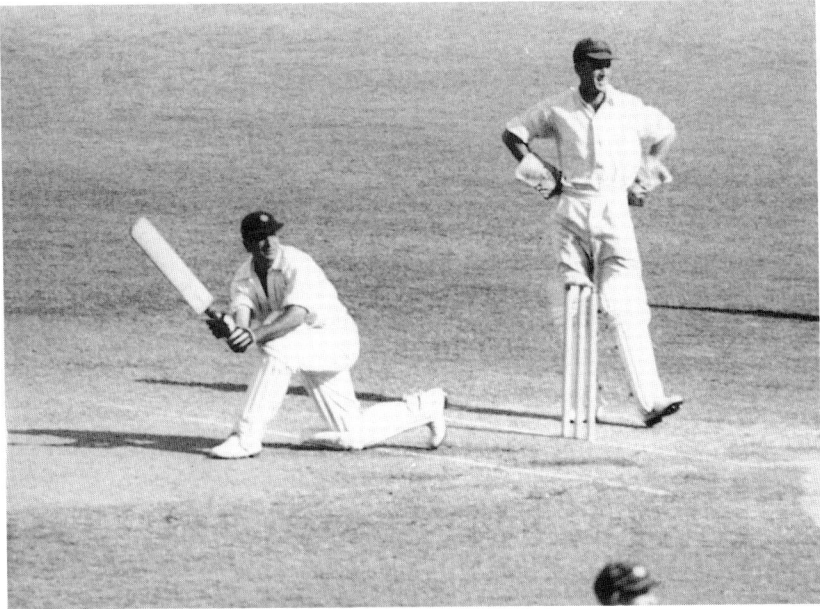

Tallon watches Vinoo Mankad lift Colin McCool over the fence in the Queensland – India match at the Gabba in November 1947 © 15

Tallon in action, 1948. Cricket writer Dick Whitington said of him: 'He strides, lithe and neatly dressed to the wicket with short, high steps, takes his place very close to the stumps. He gets very low on his heels, with elbows outside his knees, folding up like a jacknife, as he shapes to take each ball. Nervous movements of his hands indicate the coil-spring tension of the man. © 16

Tallon pretends to receive a congratulations call by phone (standard pose required by newspaper photographers) after his selection for the 1948 tour of England © 17

A familiar face: Tallon in 1948 © 18

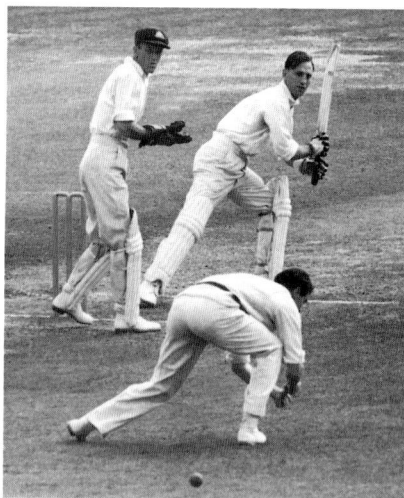

Tallon watches Keith Miller grab at and miss an edge from Len Hutton in the fifth test in 1948. Miller has expressed the view that Tallon was as supreme in wicketkeeping as Don Bradman was in batting. Alan Davidson says the same thing. 'Bradman averaged 99.94 with the bat, the next best was about 60', Davidson says. 'I have always thought of Don Tallon as being about that much better than the rest of them in keeping. Tallon was 99.94 and Wally Grout and Godfrey Evans were about 60. I put Healy up there about 60, too.' © 19

Tallon and Denis Compton in the fifth test at the Oval, 1948: Compton later wrote 'The late Wally Grout was a highly effective performer with a string of records without in my opinion matching the dazzling perfection of Don Tallon in the first two series against England after the war. Tall and lissom, Tallon was lightning in his movements. © 20

Tallon drives on the third tee at Burnham Beeches Golf Club in Buckinghamshire in 1948. It was at this club that Tallon said to have won money playing a few locals at snooker. © 21

The Australians in 1948 were invincible. Back row (from left) - Ian Johnson, Arthur Morris, Ernie Toshack, Keith Miller, Don Tallon, Ray Lindwall, Neil Harvey; Front row (from left) - Bill Brown, Lindsay Hassett, Don Bradman, Colin McCool, Sid Barnes © 22

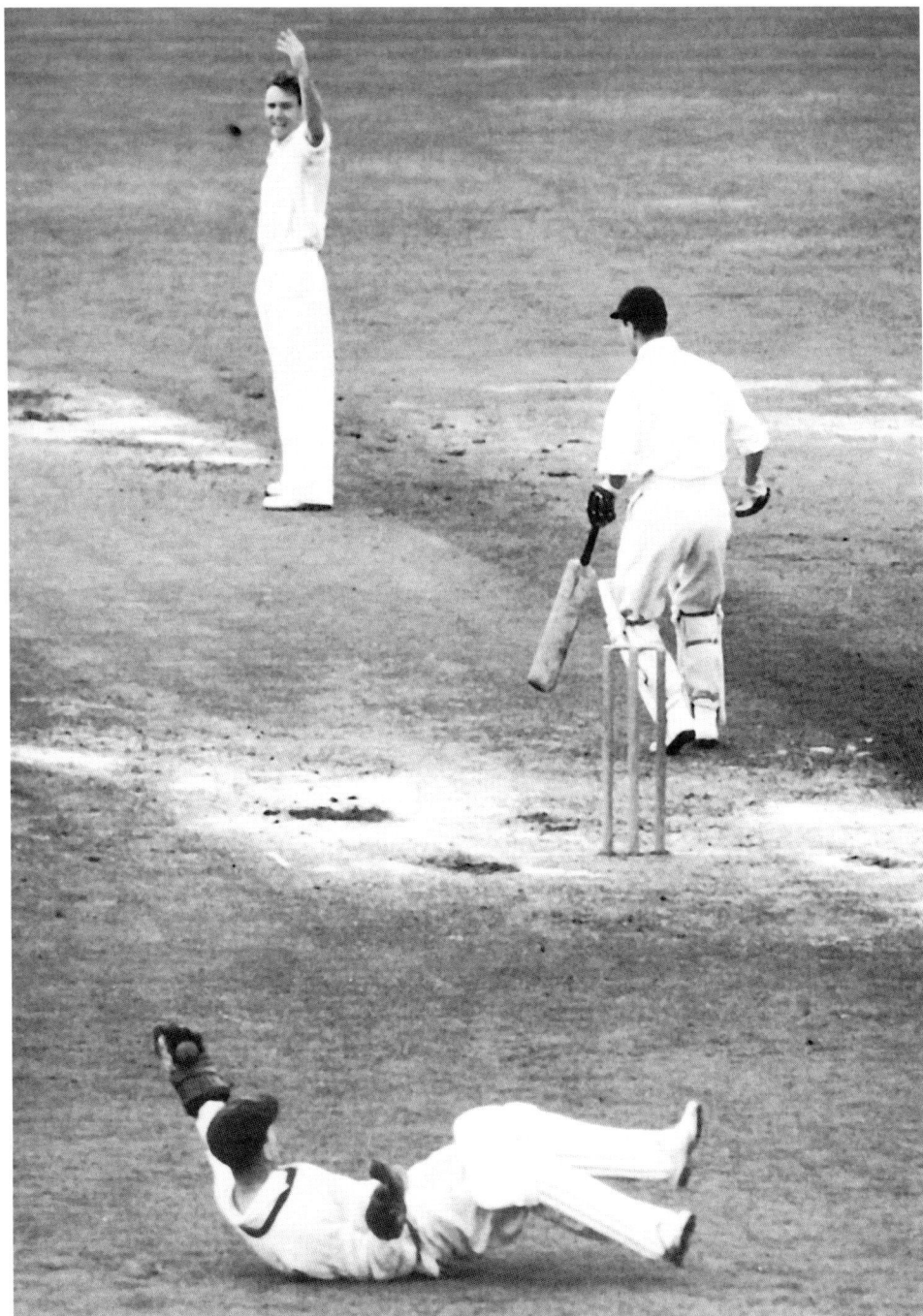

Tallon's famous leg side catch to dismiss Len Hutton off Ray Lindwall's bowling in the fifth test in 1948. Keith Miller said of it: 'I was standing in slips and to this day I cannot imagine how Tallon moved to take the catch.' © 23

Tallon (extreme right) catches the England left hander, Jack Crapp, for 0 off Miller's bowling in the fifth test in 1948. © 24

Queensland takes the field against Victoria at the Gabba, January 1949. From left, the players are: Don Tallon, Keith Jack, Ken Archer (obscured), Bill Brown, Mick Raymer, Aub Carrigan, Ken Mackay, Bill Morris (obscured), Colin McCool, Frank Nolan, Len Johnson. © 25

In England in 1953: Tallon's last Australian tour. Back row (from left) - Jim de Courcy, Colin McDonald, Gil Langley, Ian Craig, Arthur Morris, Jack Hill, Ron Archer; Middle row (from left) - Alan Davidson, Keith Miller, Graeme Hole, Richie Benaud, Doug Ring, Bill Johnson; Front row (from left) - Neil Harvey, Lindsay Hassett, Don Tallon. © 26

Tallon is applauded by the NSW players as he arrives at the crease for his final innings at the Gabba in November 1953. Tallon was rarely the batsman after the war that he had been before. Bill O'Reilly wrote after the 1950-51 Ashes series: 'Tallon at one time was a gifted strokemaker. Before the war he was quite rightly regarded as one of the best strokemakers in the game. But his batting talents have long since departed. He no longer faces up to the job with confidence, and when confidence goes all is lost.' © 27

The Tallon-Johnson juggle at Sydney in 1950-51: Len Hutton has edged the ball off Jack Iverson to Tallon, who has deflected the ball to Ian Johnson at slip, who has not held it but managed to scoop it up. Seconds later Tallon dived to take the catch. © 28

Don and Linda Tallon at their
wedding, 1954 © 29

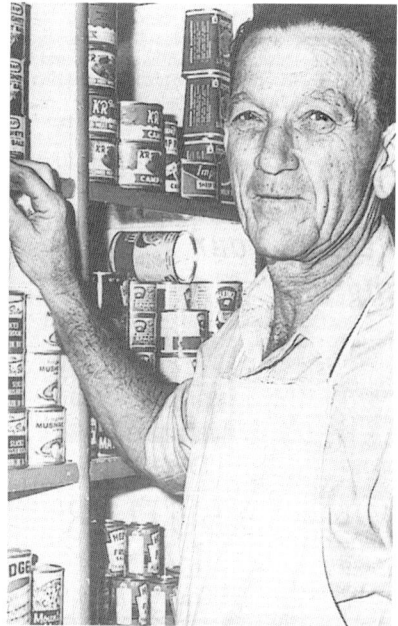

Tallon in his corner shop. © 30

Tallon bowls for Queensland at the Gabba in January 1951. Victoria's batsmen
scored 36 runs from his 29 deliveries. © 31

6

WARTIME INTERVAL

Bill Tallon was an extrovert and a noted raconteur; whose stories owed much of their humour to the fact that he had a pronounced stutter. Richie Benaud, among others, liked to collect and retell Bill Tallon's stories, many of which revolved around his brother Don. Bill is said to have been enormously proud of Don, whom he liked to refer to as 'my b-b-b-brother Donny, the international c-c-c-cricketer.'

Don Tallon was a different personality altogether. He was quiet to the point of sometimes seeming uncommunicative, slightly nervous by disposition, basically introverted, intelligent without being intellectual, devoid of any pretensions, easily swayed, unorganised, quite often late but liked by most people who knew him. Colin McCool, who roomed with Tallon while touring with both the Queensland and Australian teams, wrote: 'Don was the vague, dreamy country boy who could never make up his mind, and travel all over the world never changed him. It was a major operation for Don to make up his mind about anything, and then, having made his decision, he would just as certainly change it before the words were out of his mouth.' One writer said he spoke 'in fast, short, jerky sentences.' Others remember him mumbling rather than talking. Andy Flanagan, who wrote a book about the 1948 Ashes tour, said: 'There is no pretence or subterfuge about him. He is as you find him, a good bloke.'

Many noted the nervous strand in his make-up. Stan Sismey recalls: 'Don was a highly strung character, a rather nervous fellow. He would chain-smoke in the dressing room while waiting to go out to bat, a bundle of nerves as it were.' Sismey remembers him as man of nervous habits and quick movements who nevertheless was 'a quiet, subdued chap – he'd never be forward in anything.' Tallon seems to have struck everyone as being a man of few words. His Australian team-mate Doug Ring says: 'All he used to do was grin at you. He hardly said anything to you. He'd gamble: he and Keith Miller used to have bets on who'd hit the next four and that sort of thing. He played cards and he smoked incessantly, of course, but he rarely said anything at all. He was such a quiet fellow. He did give you advice, though. He'd come down the pitch and talk to you. I remember several times he said to me, "Give the ball more air and we'll get this fella stumped." Very perceptive but didn't talk much at all – just grinned. He was a really quiet man.' Ken Gulliver, who played for NSW against Tallon before the war, remembers the grin. 'He had an unusual temperament: nothing seemed to worry him,' Gulliver said. 'He always had something in the nature of a half-smile on his face, as though he was enjoying himself.'

Although Australia had gone to war just before the 1939-40 season, the Shield competition went ahead as normal. Tallon was again in superb form behind the stumps and had one great success with the bat, scoring 154 in 185 minutes against Victoria at the Gabba and hitting one six. (Tallon made a habit of hitting one six in each of his bigger innings.) In the previous match at the Gabba, against South Australia, Tallon had caught Don Bradman, who did not often get out in the nineties, for 97 off the bowling of Geoff Cook. It may have been this innings by Bradman (it was certainly one about this time at the Gabba) which Bill Brown remembers for another reason. Bradman had only just arrived at the crease when Cook bowled him an off-break that drifted away. Bradman went out after the ball to cover-drive it, but, seeing it drifting further way, pulled out of the stroke, spun around and put his bat back over the crease only to find that in the meantime Tallon had taken the ball, swept it to the stumps and appealed loudly for a stumping. The umpire at square leg immediately raised his finger but an instant later, with his finger still up, he began shaking his head, perhaps having realised the consequences of his original decision (a sizeable crowd has come to the Gabba to see Bradman bat). Brown, the captain, had to ask the umpire for his decision. 'Not out,' said the umpire, finally taking his finger down.

Tallon and his younger brother Matt enlisted in the Army at Bundaberg in August 1940, both joining the 47th Battalion. Until then Don had continued to work as a car salesman at Eagers in Brisbane. His Army service record lists his religion as Presbyterian and a scar on his forehead as his distinctive mark. Tallon appears to have been based initially at Maryborough but was later posted to Townsville. Although the Shield competition was abandoned in the 1940-41 season, a number of 'patriotic' interstate matches were staged around the country, and cricketers in uniform like Tallon were released to play in them. Tallon played in four such matches that summer, all of them counted as first-class, and in the second of them, Combined Queensland-Victoria versus New South Wales, he played perhaps the most brilliant innings of his career against an attack which included Bill O'Reilly. He reached 50 in 47 minutes, then raced to 100 in 84 minutes, becoming the first batsman to make a hundred before lunch in a first-class match at the Gabba. He was eventually out for 152, having hit his customary six.

Tallon played in one other first-class match in that 1940-41 season. It was a 'special patriotic match' at Melbourne between teams led by Don Bradman and Stan McCabe. The match was Clarrie Grimmett's farewell to big cricket. He played in the same team as Tallon, so at the very end of his career the old leg-spinner had the satisfaction of working with the keeper he rated above all others. Tallon did not let him down: he provided Grimmett with a stumping in each innings.

This match was played in January 1941. The next we hear of Tallon was in April that year, when he was charged with being AWOL for three days from his unit in Maryborough (perhaps he made a return trip to nearby Bundaberg). Convicted, he was fined £1 and confined to barracks for seven days. It was hardly a serious offence for a young man. Tallon, it is worth remembering, had not long before turned 25.

In the following summer, 1941-42, Tallon played in the first of what was to be a new series of patriotic matches. It was a three-day game between Queensland and NSW at the Gabba and was memorable for the fact that a 20-year-old fast bowler named Ray Lindwall made his first-class debut. This match also proved to be Stan McCabe's last first-class appearance, for following the Japanese attack on Pearl Harbour a few days later the rest of the matches were cancelled.

Tallon's military career ended abruptly in 1943. Indeed, he was fortunate his life did not end then, too. At the time he was heading north to his Army unit after playing cricket in a charity match in Brisbane and had stopped off at Bundaberg on the way home. He collapsed at Bundaberg's railway station waiting for his train and was taken by ambulance to Bundaberg Hospital, where he was found to have a ruptured duodenal ulcer. One of the doctors told his family that he was lucky medical treatment had been so close at hand. If he had collapsed a few hours later when his train was in the middle of nowhere, the doctor said, he would probably have died.

All this happened in January. Tallon spent several months convalescing, and by the time he was well enough to get about again the Army decided he was no longer fit for service. In May 1943 he was discharged. Before that happened, though, he had become romantically attached to one of the nursing sisters he met in hospital. Her name was Isabel Beattie, and she and Tallon were to marry soon after the war ended.

Tallon's brother Matt served as a machine-gunner with the 47th Battalion and went on to distinguish himself in combat in New Guinea. He was mentioned in despatches for routing Japanese snipers and machine-gun nests and won the Military Cross in Bougainville for a special act of heroism. When an enemy stronghold resisted all attempts to clear it, Matt Tallon moved out under fire, sheltered behind a disused tank and used a field telephone to direct fire onto the Japanese position until it was destroyed.

Don Tallon was 23 years old when the war began. Now, as the war began to draw to a close, he was only a couple of years off 30, but it seems the idea of hanging up his gloves did not cross his mind. Tallon had years of lost time to make up, many missed opportunities to retrieve. His ambition to play Test cricket was apparently as fierce as ever. The only question clouding the issue was whether he would still be good enough. He must have been reassured on this score in September 1944 when he appeared for a Queensland team in a fund-raising match against a side from New South Wales representing the RAAF, which included several big-name cricketers, Bill O'Reilly, Stan McCabe and Sid Barnes among them. Tallon was in fine form with both gloves and bat.

A year later the war was over and cricket began again in earnest. The first first-class match played in Australia after the war was between Queensland and NSW at the Gabba, starting on 23 November 1945, and Tallon was at his brilliant best behind the stumps. He bagged eight dismissals, four in each innings, and six of the eight were off the bowling of the leg-spinner Colin McCool, who had just transferred from NSW to Queensland. Tallon stumped three batsmen, including Sid Barnes, off McCool's bowling in the second innings, which suggested the two were somehow operating as a duo. This was true. Over the next few years Tallon and McCool were a successful and much-feared combination in Test cricket as well as in Shield. The two became good friends and roomed together. McCool, it was said, understood what made Tallon tick.

Queensland's third match of the season was against South Australia in Adelaide, and McCool took seven wickets in the first innings, no fewer than five of them jointly with Tallon. Bradman was one of their victims, although McCool could not take much credit for that. Here is Mick Raymer's account of the dismissal: 'Colin McCool bowled Bradman a terrible ball – it nearly bounced twice before it got to him – and Bradman chased it to first slip, trying to cut it, and Don Tallon took the catch right off the end of Bradman's bat, two inches off the ground. That's how good Tallon was. He was a freak.'

Tallon's batting form was good, too. He again topped the Brisbane grade averages in 1945-46, admittedly aided by not outs. He batted six times, was out only twice, had a top score of 109 not out and scored a total of 239 runs for an average of 119.50.

Half-way through the season the Brisbane Telegraph's cricket writer, N V Stock, declared that, whereas Tallon's omission from the 1938 side had been met merely with general indignation, his omission now would cause a public outcry that would rock the cricket world. In fact, the cricket world was in no danger of being rocked. Tallon was almost certainly one of the first players chosen for the Australian team that toured New Zealand in March 1946. He had just turned 30.

7
ON TOP AT LAST

The war robbed Don Tallon of his best years, as it did so many other cricketers of his generation, and when it was over he was left with only a short time at the top. Fortunately, Tallon made the most of that time. Now past 30, he was no longer the fresh-faced tyro we see in pre-war photographs. In the intervening years he had developed the lined, leathery features which were to become familiar to cricket followers everywhere. His skill, though, had lost none of its edge. On the five-match tour of New Zealand in March 1946, he showed some patchy form in earlier matches, but his keeping in the one Test of the tour in Wellington, Tallon's debut Test, was outstanding. Mervyn Fenn, who covered the tour for the Sydney Morning Herald, singled out Tallon in his tour summary as one of the star performers, noting that 'every member of the team is delighted with Tallon's superb keeping in the Test.' This match was the last of Bill O'Reilly's 27 Tests. O'Reilly bowled his leg-breaks at a lively medium pace which made it harder for him to get batsmen stumped, so much so that in all his previous 26 Tests (Bert Oldfield was the keeper in most of them) O'Reilly had had only one stumping. Tallon kept to O'Reilly in just this one Test, yet he managed to stump one batsman and, but for the umpire, ought to have stumped a second.

The story about this other, disallowed stumping was told by Ray Lindwall in his autobiography. Lindwall said he was fielding at short square-leg when Tallon stumped a New Zealander off O'Reilly's bowling. He did it with such speed, Lindwall said, that it was almost too fast for the eye to see, but it was unquestionably a stumping: the batsman was a good six inches out of his crease. Yet the umpire turned down the appeal. Surprised by the decision, Lindwall asked the umpire about it at the end of the over. He replied with unusual candour. 'He was just too quick for me,' he said. 'He did it all with such speed that I didn't know whether he took the ball in front or level with the stumps. I just had to give the batsman the benefit of the doubt.'

The following summer, 1946-47, brought the long-awaited resumption of Ashes cricket. The England team that toured that year encountered Tallon for the first time in the match against Queensland at the Gabba. It was a chastening experience, for England's batsmen proved easy prey for the Tallon-McCool pincer. McCool took nine wickets in the match, and Tallon, who was captaining Queensland, was responsible for six of them, stumping four and catching two. Denis Compton, who played in the match, wrote: 'We had all heard of his prowess as a stumper and were to find that he was not overrated, as are many sportsmen.' Tallon and McCool had other successes against the Englishmen in the Tests that followed. In the fifth Test at Sydney, for instance, Tallon stumped three off McCool's bowling in England's second innings. Bruce Harris, an English journalist who covered the tour, wrote later: 'Tallon is an aggressive wicketkeeper. I have heard our batsmen say that the knowledge that he is behind the stumps to his fellow Queenslander McCool is always on their minds.'

The most talked-about Tallon-McCool dismissal that series was a catch Tallon took in the second Test at Sydney to dismiss Denis Compton. McCool pitched a leg-break outside the off stump which Compton tried to drive but edged. The ball flew sharply to Ian Johnson at slip, struck him in the chest and dropped to the ground. In that instant Tallon turned, saw the ball falling and threw himself backwards, just managing to shoot a glove under it before it hit the ground. Ray Robinson, who witnessed the catch, said: 'Such speed of mind and action seems incredible. Only the world's greatest keeper could have done it.'

McCool was not the only leg-spinner in the Australian team. In the first two Tests and in the fifth the other leg-spinner was the Victorian George Tribe, who bowled a wrong'un batsmen found hard to pick. Before the first Test Don Bradman asked Tallon if he could pick Tribe's wrong'un, adding for emphasis: 'We don't want Hammond halfway down the wicket and you going the wrong way.' Alarmed, Tallon got Tribe to bowl to him. It was, Tallon said later, the only time he ever practised taking a bowler. Needless to say, Tallon did not find Tribe's wrong'un a problem.

In the opinion of virtually everyone who saw him then, Tallon's keeping in 1946-47 was a marvel, at once brilliant and safe. He finished the series with 20 dismissals, an Australian record. England's batsmen soon became conscious of the danger that lay behind them whenever they took guard. As the England keeper Godfrey Evans wrote: 'I know many England batsmen felt a sense of impending woe when Don was behind the stumps.' Tallon's keeping that summer made a lasting impression on Evans, who for as long as he lived would speak of it as representing the pinnacle of the art. Evans made the following note on Tallon's method: 'He moved to take the ball late, not committing himself until he had watched for any movement of the pitch and would remain largely unnoticed – a sure sign of a high-class wicketkeeper. Then, quite suddenly when spotting a chance, he would fling himself to take a catch or remove the bails in an instant . . . He was equally adept standing back or standing up, which he frequently did to bowlers of medium pace and above, and his gathering of returns was magnificent. His excellence inspired both bowlers and fieldsmen.'

Evans was brought into the England side for the second Test, and he took the unusual step of going into the Australian dressing room to ask Tallon for advice, which Tallon was prepared to give. 'I thought there was no harm in talking to him,' Tallon recalled. The word in the Australian camp was that Evans was not much of a keeper, anyway, so Tallon felt he could afford to patronise him. By the end of the series he might not have been so generous. By then the Australians had come to regard Evans as one of the England team's finest players.

This second Test was the first of Ian Johnson's career, and he had success in his very first over, dismissing Len Hutton for 39, caught behind on the legside by Tallon. In an interview long afterwards, Tallon rated this as one of his better catches, his reason being that Hutton had glanced the ball off the middle of the bat. Tallon told a story about this dismissal in another interview. He said he had noticed before lunch that Hutton was playing at deliveries from Ernie Toshack just outside the leg stump. 'I kept thinking to myself I'm going to get this fellow here soon,' he said. During the lunch break Tallon told the other Australians of his observation, and immediately after lunch Bradman brought on Johnson. "Len played at it and this time it didn't miss his bat, and I caught it. I think I got so excited about it that before I had finished appealing I was standing nearly on the square leg umpire.'

There were a few negative comments, most of them about Tallon's appealing. Compton thought he made too many appeals for catches that were obviously not going to be given and he implied Tallon did it to upset the batsmen. He thought this was a counter-productive ploy, because umpires would soon work him out. In his book about the series Clif Cary blamed Tallon's impetuous appealing for what some judged to be Washbrook's unfair dismissal, caught behind, in the fourth Test. Cary was told Tallon admitted at once that it had not been a catch, yet Washbrook was not recalled. Cary also criticised Tallon for being over-eager in covering balls wide on the offside, thereby obstructing first slip's view of the ball. Cary said this cost Australia at least one wicket in the series.

Compton had one other criticism of Tallon. 'I think he is inclined to overdo the showmanship,' he said. 'Don Tallon is the idol of the crowd, although his spectacular type of wicketkeeping might not prove so popular in England.' It is hard to imagine what Compton meant by this, for Tallon was hardly the flamboyant type. On the contrary: it seems to have been a characteristic of his keeping style that he remained largely inconspicuous until a chance came along and he suddenly went into action. Perhaps it was merely his extroverted appealing which Compton had in mind.

Tallon produced one memorable performance with the bat. In the third Test at Melbourne he and Ray Lindwall made a spectacular assault on the England bowling, scoring 154 between them for the eighth wicket in 88 minutes. A G 'Johnnie' Moyes described this partnership as 'one of the finest pieces of sustained hitting ever seen in a Test match.' Tallon raced to 90 at high speed but then, apparently losing his nerve, began playing cautiously and was caught and bowled by Doug Wright for 92, scored in 105 minutes. It was the closest he ever came to making a Test century. Lindwall was more fortunate, going on to make exactly 100.

India toured the following summer, 1947-48, and Tallon played in all five Tests. His keeping was again top-class. Bill Johnston made the Australian team in this series and got to know Tallon as a keeper. Tallon used to stand back to Johnston's medium-fast bowling when the ball was new and swinging, but when the ball was older he often stood up to him – and he always stood up if any batsman dared take guard outside the crease. 'He wouldn't tell me he was going to stand up – he'd just get up there,' Johnston said. 'His taking on the legside was just fantastic, especially when I bowled one of my faster ones that he didn't expect and it went down the legside. He'd take it so cleanly – I used to wonder how he did it.'

Tallon had a poor series with the bat, scoring just 49 runs in five innings at an average of 12.25. It was a common observation that Tallon after the war was not the batsman he had been before. A G 'Johnnie' Moyes had an explanation for this: 'The post-war generation never really knew just how splendid a batsman-wicketkeeper Don Tallon was, for after the war he forgot that he had made his name as a driver and relied far too much on prods and pushes, which brought fewer runs and less joy to Tallon and onlookers.' Tallon's decline as a batsman was not really so surprising. Keeping at the top level demands such intense concentration over such long periods that keepers do not have much mental energy left to apply to their batting, which is surely why so few of them in history have performed consistently with the bat.

In early March 1948, a few weeks after the final Test against India, Tallon went into hospital at Bundaberg to have his tonsils removed. It seems he had bothered by sore throats for some time and, after a medical examination, was directed by the Board of Control, as the Australian Cricket Board was then known, to have the operation. Tallon had been chosen in the Australian side that was about to leave for a tour of England, and the board did not want him getting sick there. Tallon joined his team-mates at Perth in mid-March, just before they sailed to England.

8
1948

The Australians' 1948 tour of England was to become one of cricket's great success stories, and the brilliance of Tallon's keeping was an important factor in that success. In the Tests he took catches which his team-mates, who knew what he was capable of, found astonishing. The most publicised of them was the legside catch he took to dismiss Len Hutton off Lindwall's bowling in the fifth Test at the Oval. Hutton glanced the ball and Tallon, diving, caught it as it was flying towards fine leg. Neil Harvey was fielding on the boundary there at the time. 'I saw the ball coming between me and Tallon, and I started running around the boundary to cut it off,' he says. 'I looked up: there was no ball and Don Tallon was half-way towards square leg with the ball in his left hand.' In a book he wrote about the series John Arlott said: 'It would have been a brilliant catch made by a bare-handed fieldsman unhampered by pads – for a man padded and gloved it was memorable – and no other wicketkeeper in the world, I fancy, could have made it a chance.' According to Arlott, Tallon moved about three yards to take the ball and caught it a bare two inches (about 5 cm) above the ground.

Tallon took another sensational catch to dismiss George Emmett in the third Test at Old Trafford, which his captain, Bradman, later described as 'one of the grandest low and wide right-hand catches ever seen in Test cricket'. Among the Australian players, though, the catch which caused most amazement was one which spectators may hardly have noticed. Even today, when you speak to veterans of the 1948 tour about Tallon, you find this catch is the one they still marvel at. It was the second Test at Lord's, and the England opener Cyril Washbrook was facing Ernie Toshack. Here is Neil Harvey's description of what followed: 'Tallon was standing over the top to Toshack, who bowled an uncharacteristic full toss – Tosh never bowled full tosses – and I think he caught Washbrook by surprise. Tosh was medium-pace, but Don always stood over the top to him. Anyway, Washbrook went back on the back foot to slam him over towards Father Time. He got an inside edge, and Don caught it at his boot tops. Off a full toss! It was one of those freak things I've never seen anyone else do.' Bradman called it 'one of the most remarkable catches ever made behind the wicket.' He wrote: 'Miraculously, Tallon got his gloves under what was to him practically a yorker. I cannot remember a similar catch. Wicketkeepers are not expected to perform miracles.'

Touring did not come easily to Tallon. He did not like packing and unpacking, and avoided the problem by living out of his suitcase. Moreover, being reserved by nature, he did not enjoy group socialising. Harvey recalls: 'He kept to himself a bit. He wasn't the most outgoing of guys, you know, but he was popular. He seemed to be a guy who got friendly with one guy in particular on a tour and stuck with him rather than share the wealth around so to speak.'

Tallon's favourite pastime was gambling. He bet on the races, and he and Keith Miller played two-up. One game in the Australian dressing room went for so long that the noise of the coins on the floor began to wear on the other players' nerves. Bradman told them to stop, but instead they laid a blanket on the floor to deaden the sound and kept playing. Tallon is said to have accepted a challenge from two locals at a golf club in Buckinghamshire to play snooker for ten shillings a corner – although only after he was offered a three-blacks start. Tallon potted balls from everywhere and pocketed the winnings.

It was supposedly on the 1948 tour that Tallon acquired the nickname 'Deafie' by which he was known for the rest of his life. A newspaper report later sourced it to an incident in a county match. All the Australian players close to the wicket except Tallon heard what they thought was a snick and all but Tallon appealed for a catch. When the umpire ruled the batsman out, Tallon said to those around him that he thought it was a rough decision, whereupon one of the fielders, Ron Hamence, retorted: 'What's the matter with you these days? You must be deaf as well as dumb.'

An injured finger kept Tallon out of fourth Test, the first he had missed since becoming Australia's keeper. As usual, too, he had occasional bad days behind the stumps. In the third Test he missed Compton not once but twice. He dropped him off Lindwall when the batsman was 50, a chance wide to the right, and he missed him again off Bill Johnston on the last ball of the day. On the whole, though, his keeping in 1948 was of the highest class, a fact that Wisden acknowledged by naming him as one of its five cricketers of the year. His opposite number in the England team, Godfrey Evans, had a fine series, too. Indeed, as he later wrote, Evans felt he came as close to perfecting his technique in 1948 as he ever would. Yet he admitted: 'Even so, I found there were still things to be learnt from Don Tallon.'

The season which followed at home, 1948-49, was Don Bradman's last, and Tallon played a starring role in Bradman's testimonial match at Melbourne in December. The match was between teams led by Bradman and Lindsay Hassett, and Tallon played for the former. On the final day, Bradman's XI was 7 for 210, trailing by 192 runs, when Tallon arrived at the crease and proceeded to play what Bradman later described as the finest innings he ever saw Tallon play. Tallon thrashed the bowling, scoring 128 in the final session. When Bruce Dooland began the last over of the match, Bradman's team needed 13 runs to win. With one ball to go, three were needed. Tallon pulled it hard to square leg and ran two, which meant the match ended in a tie. Tallon was undefeated on 146. Bradman wrote there was much excitement in the dressing room as in a Test match. 'When he came into the dressing room,' Bradman said, 'Don was so excited that he honestly did not know whether we had won or not.'

9

OFF THE BOIL

The triumphs of the 1948 Ashes tour were still fresh in people's minds when Don Tallon's cricket career took a strange turn. Before the 1949-50 season he made two decisions which surprised everyone. First, he ruled himself out of the Australian tour of South Africa that summer. Second, he announced to the Queensland selectors that he would not be available as a wicketkeeper but was ready and willing to play for the state as a leg-spin bowler. Clearly, for reasons of his own, Tallon felt he needed a break from what he had been doing.

What were those reasons? The one offered to journalists curious to know why he could not go to South Africa was that he had opened a sport store in Bundaberg in partnership with a local man, Norm Smith, and could not afford to be out of the country again for months so soon after the 1948 tour of England. This explanation was not entirely convincing, though, for the business would surely have benefited from his continuing presence in the Australian team. Another story which did the rounds among his Queensland team-mates was that he was talked into pulling out of the tour by someone who persuaded him (Tallon was notoriously easy to persuade) that he would gain some tax benefit by not touring. There may have been other factors. It seems his marriage was by now under strain, and his health may well have been indifferent, too. It is also possible he felt that for the time being he had simply had enough of the constant stress, both mental and physical, of keeping wickets at the top level. His hands were becoming increasingly prone to damage, an indication that his timing was not quite what it had been.

His friend Colin McCool said he spent hours pleading with Tallon to change his mind about South Africa. 'I hated to see him damaging his cricket future this way.' McCool said. But for once Tallon would not be moved. According to another, quite different account, Tallon was selected in the original side, decided to withdraw, changed his mind after persuasion from friends and asked to be reinstated but was told by the selectors that his place had already been filled by Gil Langley.

His unwillingness to keep for Queensland was even more peculiar. The first Shield match of the season was against NSW at the Gabba, and Tallon made himself available only as a spin bowler. Tallon loved to bowl and had a high opinion of his own bowling, yet it is hard to see how he could seriously have expected to be chosen in the state side as a bowler-batsman. Perhaps he had been encouraged by his bowling form in early-season club matches in Bundaberg. A fortnight earlier he had taken 7 for 61 for Past Highs in a match against Railways. The Queensland selectors were not interested. They called Tallon's bluff, left him out of the team and played Grout in his place. Grout was contacted by the Queensland selector Rex Rogers, who told him: 'Tallon wants to bowl and we are not going to pick him.' This proved to be Grout's only appearance for Queensland that summer. Tallon 'took the hint', as Grout later expressed it, and returned to his place behind the stumps.

Tallon did bowl for Queensland that season, though. In a match against South Australia at Adelaide two months later, he was asked to bowl by his captain, Bill Brown, after one of the side's spinners, Allan Young, hurt a finger. The all-rounder Aub Carrigan took over the gloves. Tallon had no success. It seems that when the ball was put in his hands Tallon suffered stage fright. Noticing there was something wrong, Brown asked him what was the matter. Tallon replied, 'I can't remember which foot I start off with.' Tallon told the same story in an interview long after he retired. 'You know what happened?' he said. 'I lost my step. There I was, after bowling a lot in club matches in Bundaberg, and I didn't know where to put my feet!'

Tallon bowled again against Victoria at the Gabba in the following season. The Victorians needed to make only 73 in their second innings to win the match and, when the Queensland opening bowlers failed to make a breakthrough, Tallon, now captain, brought himself on to bowl and gave the gloves to, of all people, McCool. He bowled 29 balls, many of them long hops and full tosses, from which the Victorians helped themselves to 36 runs.

Tallon began the 1950-51 season as captain of Queensland, Bill Brown having retired, and in Queensland's second match, against NSW in Sydney, he miscalculated badly with what was really his first important captaincy decision. It was the day of the Melbourne Cup and also the last day of the match, which looked to be tailing off into a draw. Queensland was scoring heavily in its second innings and appeared to have made the match safe when the NSW captain, Arthur Morris, urged Tallon to take a chance on winning by declaring. It was also suggested to him (by Keith Miller, according to one account) that the declaration should be made in time for both teams to listen to the Melbourne Cup broadcast. The NSW bowlers made Tallon's decision easier by serving up easy deliveries to Queensland's Mick Harvey, who was nearing a century. As soon as Harvey reached his century, Tallon closed the innings, whereupon the players ran from the field to listen to the race on the radio.

Because there was then just over two hours' play left, Tallon's declaration seemed a safe gamble. In the event, Morris and Miller opened NSW's second innings and attacked the bowling with such gusto that they scored the 225 runs needed to win the match with 11 minutes to spare. Miller made 138 not out and Morris, who let his partner have his head, 78 not out in 119 minutes.

Ray Robinson must have studied Tallon closely before penning this portrait of him in action in 1950: 'Tallon is the Paganini of wicketkeepers,' he wrote. 'You see this first in the mystic passes his gloves make before the bowler begins: he gives occult signals by wriggling his fingers; with elbows close to his body he draws his hands sinuously down in front of his chest. He stands nearer the stumps than the others – stands guard over them, alert as a sentry, left foot behind the middle stump. As an outlet for nervous energy his feet smooth down the already-level ground. He puts his wrists against his hips, then wipes his forehead with the strip of bare forearm between gauntlet and shirtsleeve. Taking the peak in both hands he resettles the cap on his curly, brown head, tugging it nearer his eyes. He stretches his shoulders, hitches his trousers' waistband, stoops half-way, then folds like a pocket-knife until legs, thighs and body seem all one piece, balanced on level feet. Though rather tall, he squats nearer his heels than the others, with elbows outside his knees. He raps the earth with his fists, makes a final pass before his face with open gloves, and peers past his right forefinger before he poises his hands in front of his shins as the bowler runs up. He crouches there, motionless, until his eyes read the ball's secret.'

England toured Australia in 1950-51 and Tallon played in all five Tests. In the first Test he leapt to take a high and wide return from Bill Johnston on the boundary, then threw down the wicket from 10 yards away as Arthur McIntyre was going for a fourth run. Godfrey Evans, the other batsman, wrote years later that this run-out was etched on his memory, for it provided 'a perfect illustration of Tallon's genius'. In the third Test at Sydney Tallon and Ian Johnson at slip shared in a juggling act similar to the one they performed on the same ground four years earlier. Len Hutton edged Jack Iverson to Tallon who deflected the ball to Johnson, who failed to hold it but did manage to scoop it up, whereupon Tallon dived backwards and caught it before it hit the ground. Neville Cardus, who was there, wrote: ' It was all very hard to follow; cricket swift and agile as a whole tree full of monkeys!'

The prevailing view, though, was that, at 34 years of age, Tallon had slipped from the heights he had previously occupied. He was now making mistakes he wouldn't have made before. In the fourth Test at Adelaide he missed a wide stumping chance off Johnson's bowling. It was costly mistake, for the batsman, Len Hutton, who was then 34, went on to carry his bat for 156 not out. Bill O'Reilly saw it as a 'simple' chance. He wrote: 'Hutton had gone well down the wicket, four to five feet, and missed a cutter which turned away from him. Tallon dropped the ball and Hutton scrambled home.'

It was probably no coincidence that Tallon's ulcer problem was particularly bad during this Test in Adelaide. Ken Archer can testify to this, for he roomed with him during the Test and saw at first hand how much he suffered. Tallon would wake during the night groaning, whereupon Archer would get up and ask, 'What's the matter, mate?', to which Tallon replied, 'I feel crook.' Archer then helped him find and take the bismuth preparation that was meant to relieve the pain. Archer is sure Tallon's condition affected his play, and he says Tallon himself was very conscious of this. After this Test, Tallon expected to be dropped and wished Archer luck for the fifth Test. As it turned out, Archer was dropped and Tallon kept his place.

Jack Fingleton had no doubt Tallon lost his edge in 1950-51. 'Tallon was not the great wicketkeeper that England knew in 1948 or that we knew four years before against Hammond's team,' he wrote in a book about the series. 'He missed a number of chances and his batting was not to be compared with four years before . . . Whatever the cause, Tallon fell below his best.' Fingleton did add: 'He was still our best man in Australia by a long way. One trouble with Tallon was that he had set such a high standard in the two previous series.' England's E W Swanton, too, saw a decline, noting that 'Tallon was only a shadow of his old self behind the wicket.'

Bill O'Reilly suggested Tallon had suffered a kind of burn-out. 'Don Tallon has lost the keen edge of his enthusiasm for the job,' he wrote, 'and consequently was never up to the magnificent standard he set in the previous two Test series. I have never seen a better keeper than Tallon as he was in England in 1948. The speed with which he carried out his stumpings had to be seen to be believed. But that time has passed. Evans is now the world's best.' O'Reilly wondered whether Tallon, after such a disappointing season, might hang up his gloves.

Tallon's career may have gone off the boil, but he had lost none of his appetite for the game. The Adelaide Test began on a Friday and did not end until the following Thursday. Tallon flew from Adelaide on the following day, Friday, but, plane connections then being what they were, did not land in Bundaberg until Saturday afternoon. Yet the very next day, Sunday, he turned out for his Bundaberg club, Past Highs, in what was said to be a vital premiership match against Railways. Although 'obviously tired from travelling,' the local News Mail said, he won the match almost single-handedly, scoring 77 and taking 9 wickets for 50.

The West Indians toured in the following summer, 1951-52, but before they arrived the old enemy within, Tallon's ulcers, finally got the better of him. He collapsed in September with a haemorrhage and was taken to

Bundaberg Hospital, where he was given a blood transfusion. One newspaper reported him as 'seriously ill.' Tallon was given a second transfusion and a couple of days later his condition was said to have improved, although his doctor was quoted as saying he faced a long convalescence, which meant he would out of big cricket for the season. Three days after he left hospital in October his club, Past Highs, began its opening club match of the season. Tallon could not resist playing. The News Mail in Bundaberg explained: 'Tallon himself hardly expected to play so soon after his illness, but he felt so well that he decided to take the field. With big matches in view this season, he is anxious to get into top form as early as possible.'

But Tallon played no first-class cricket that season. Gil Langley replaced him in the Australian side and Wally Grout, who had previously played only seven matches for Queensland in five seasons, kept for Queensland. As Grout later admitted, he had sometimes despaired of ever securing the job permanently, and at the very outset of his first-class career he considered moving to South Australia. What deterred him, ironically, was an announcement in the press in early 1947 that Tallon was going there, too. Tallon was reported to have accepted a job running an Adelaide hotel, which naturally meant he would thereafter play for South Australia. So Grout decided to remain in Queensland, only to find later that Tallon had changed his mind and would stay there, too.

10
FADE OUT

After a year out of the spotlight, Tallon was ready to return to big cricket in 1952-53. Grout had to make way for him in the Queensland side, but the Australian selectors chose to persevere with Langley for the Tests against South Africa. Technically, because Tallon was not the incumbent keeper, he had not been dropped, but this was what the selectors' decision amounted to. Before the first Test the touring South Africans came to Bundaberg to play Queensland Country. Perhaps because the match was being played in his home town, Tallon agreed to lead the country team and performed well behind the stumps, catching four South Africans in one innings. Two days later Tallon played against the South Africans again, this time for Queensland at the Gabba. Taking advantage of two let-offs, he scored a bright 133, advancing from 66 to 94 with seven successive boundaries. Johnnie Moyes wrote that this 'was his most noble innings since the 1946-47 season, a scene of rare sparkle, with drives cutting through the field, almost burning the grass with their brilliance.'

By now, though, it had been announced that Langley had kept his place in the Australian team for the opening Test. When Tallon reached his century he was given a huge ovation, which those who were there took to be partly in sympathy at being left out of the Test side. Some of the crowd also shouted insults at the national selector Jack Ryder when he took his seat in the Members' Stand. Johnnie Moyes, who knew Ryder well, said, 'That genial soul was not disturbed by the outburst.'

As it happened, there was a Queenslander on the selection panel, Bill Brown, but there was a South Australian, Phil Ridings, on it, too, and to Queensland minds it seemed that Ridings and the third selector, Ryder of Victoria, had conspired to replace the northerner, Tallon, with a southerner, Langley. There were six Victorians in the eleven, three New South Welshmen, two South Australians – and no Queenslanders. Queenslanders believed there ought to have been two in the side, Tallon and McCool. Some non-Queenslanders thought to, too. In a book they wrote jointly, Dick Whitington and Keith Miller said that Tallon's and McCool's performances that season 'were at least as good (actually better than) Langley's and Johnson's.'

During the first Test at the Gabba spectators continued to express resentment. They jeered at Langley and generally singled out Victorian players for abuse. Ian Johnson, whom many Queenslanders regarded as occupying McCool's rightful place in the side, received a blast of derision when he dropped a catch in slips. Langley, an overnight batsman, was out at the start of play on the second morning and the crowd hooted with delight. Later that day Langley missed a stumping chance off Johnson's bowling, an error that resulted in a chorus of abuse and jeering. 'Where's Tallon?' spectators called. 'Bring back Tallon.' Richie Benaud, Australia's 12th man, observed all this from the dressing room. He recalled in his 1998 autobiography: 'Fortunately for him [Langley] there were only 10,000 there that day, although they made the noise of 30,000.' Wally Grout, a spectator sitting among the barrackers on the Gabba hill, felt for Langley, for he knew that the delivery he failed to take from Johnson, a full-pitched off-break, was one of the hardest for any keeper to handle. Grout stood up, like 'a Hyde Park orator' as he later described it, and spoke in Langley's defence to those around him, saying, 'You mugs wouldn't know,' or words to that effect.

Johnnie Moyes was horrified at the demonstration – and at reports that many Queenslanders were boycotting the Test in protest – all of which, he said, strengthened the case of those who wanted the Brisbane Test given to Perth. 'It was all rather sad and not in the spirit of cricket,' he said. At the same time, Moyes felt some sympathy for Tallon. 'Reports by some competent judges were that he seemed as good as ever,' he wrote. 'If so, he was the best in the land.'

In fact, Tallon did have a successful season. In eight matches for Queensland he caught 24 and stumped nine – and five of those stumpings were in combination with his old partner McCool. This was why, in spite of his advanced age (he was now 37), the selectors picked him for the tour of England in 1953. Whatever may have been thought in hindsight about his inclusion in the team, the truth is Tallon deserved his place at the time the side was chosen.

The 1953 tour was an unhappy one for Tallon. For a while all went well. His form was good – good enough to be chosen ahead of Langley for the first Test at Trent Bridge. In early tour matches he is said to have complained of claustrophobia, meaning that first slip and leg slip, who were standing where they had become accustomed to standing for Langley, were too close. Tallon wanted them wider.

There was a humorous misunderstanding involving Tallon during the first Test. On a difficult pitch in poor light Australia's batting collapsed in the second innings, and as the wickets tumbled the Australian captain, Lindsay Hassett, spoke to the other players in the dressing room about the possibility of appealing against the light. Tallon was sitting there with his pads on but apparently did not listen to what was said. When the sixth wicket fell for 81 and Tallon rose to go out to bat, Hassett told him to 'give

46

it a go', meaning to appeal against the light. Tallon thought he meant have a go at the bowling, which is what he proceeded to do, much to the amazement of his team-mates watching from the dressing room. Hitting out, he raced to 15 before being caught in the outfield. Although conceived in error, Tallon's do-or-die policy was actually not a bad one, for his 15 proved to be the second highest score of the innings and helped ensure a draw.

This was to be Tallon's only Test on the tour and, indeed, the last Test of his career. For the rest of the tour he was to be Langley's deputy, a role he did not enjoy. Arthur Morris, one of the selection panel which dropped him, recalls: 'I remember it upset Don very much.' Asked why Tallon had been chosen for the first Test, Morris said, 'I suppose we were hoping that when it came to the Test match Don would be at his dazzling best again. He wasn't.' Like other team-mates, Morris thought Tallon might have retired earlier. 'I rate him the best keeper I ever saw,' Morris said. 'He was brilliant. Mobility was his great thing: mobility behind the stumps – quick feet, quick movements, quick reflexes, quick into position. Bertie Oldfield was a great keeper, but he went on too long. I think Don went on a bit too long, too.'

It is likely that Tallon's age and state of health both contributed to his decline. Tallon admitted this in an interview with Alan Trengrove in 1965. 'I was feeling a bit crook . . . my ulcer played havoc with me,' he said. 'My eyes were going, too. Once you start fumbling the ball you know you've had it.' He said the ball was starting to hurt his hands, a sign he had lost his timing and was tensing up. 'I was getting nervous, lifting my chin and taking my eyes off the ball,' he said. 'It was the end of the road.'

There was another factor which may have affected his performance. In May, a few weeks after the tour began, Tallon's lawyer began divorce proceedings on his behalf against his wife, Isabel. The marriage break-up is said to have been stressful for everyone concerned and must have weighed on Tallon's mind.

Whatever the reason, Tallon was a rather forlorn figure for the rest of his time in England. He appeared to have resigned himself to being a passenger on the tour and behaved accordingly. Jack Fingleton wrote: 'Tallon, after a good showing in the first Test, seemed to lose all interest. It was a tragedy to see such a great man fall, and be prepared to fall, on such evil days.' During the fourth Test at Leeds the Australians stayed at a hotel in the nearby town of Harrogate, and on one or more days of the Test Tallon remained in the hotel instead of going to the match. Fingleton noted this and criticised him for it, although it seems the real reason for Tallon's absence was that he was suffering with his ulcer. Neil Harvey says: 'Don was gone in '53. You could see in his own play, in his own approach to the game, that he'd lost his enthusiasm, that he knew he was on the way out. He probably shouldn't have gone on that tour. On reflection it was a bad selection.'

On the day after the fourth Test ended at Leeds, Tallon made news by helping to rescue a man whose truck had caught fire on the Great North Road at Highgate in the north of London. According to a newspaper report, Tallon was a passenger in a car heading towards London. When the truck driver jumped out of the blazing cabin with his clothes alight, Tallon and the unnamed driver of the car helped smother the flames with grass. The truck driver escaped with burns to one leg.

The 1953 tour might have been the end, but Tallon was not quite finished. Before the 1953-54 season began, he declared his intention to keep playing. Wally Grout, who had been expecting him to retire, heard the announcement on a lunchtime news bulletin and 'nearly choked on my carrots'. Grout need not have worried. The first game of the season, against NSW at the Gabba, was to be Tallon's last for Queensland. On the second day of the match he had a health scare and young Peter Burge replaced him behind the stumps. The press was told Tallon had hurt a finger, but there was another reason. This is Burge's account of what happened: 'Straight after lunch – he'd had a drink of raspberry soft drink – he had a bit of a spit, saw it was red and thought he was haemorrhaging. I took the gloves from him. I'll never forget those gloves. There wasn't even any rubber on them.'

This was on the Saturday of the match. On Monday Tallon announced he was retiring. No explanation was offered, although Tallon did tell a reporter he had all but made up his mind before the game that this would be his farewell. This was true. Bill Brown, a selector at the time, says that Tallon had asked to be chosen for this match on the understanding it would be his farewell. He told the selectors he wanted to retire, not be dropped, and the selectors were happy to go along with this. On Tuesday, the last day of the match, Tallon went out in style, scoring 54 not out, including nine fours, in 35 minutes. The match was heading for a draw, so the opposing captain, Keith Miller, knowing this was Tallon's last appearance, made it easy for him. He brought on Jim Burke who bowled a series of half-volleys, and Tallon hit four boundaries in four balls. After he passed 50 the Queensland captain, Ken Archer, closed the innings, not wishing to impose too much on Miller's generosity. On returning to the dressing room Tallon complained to him: 'Why did you declare? I could have scored a century.'

A few weeks later the Queensland Cricket Association launched a public subscription for Tallon with a £250 donation of its own. The association considered staging a testimonial match for him, but decided not to for several reasons, the main one being that the costs involved would make it a doubtful proposition financially. In Melbourne, though, a testimonial match was staged in January 1954 for Lindsay Hassett, who was also retiring, and Tallon agreed to play in it. It was his final first-class appearance. Tallon managed just one dismissal, and appropriately it was a stumping: he stumped Neil Harvey off Richie Benaud's bowling. Hassett made 126 in the same innings, and he had Tallon to thank for this. Len Maddocks, who was to become Australia's keeper later that year, watched the match. He says: 'When Hassett first came in he leg-glanced somebody, and Tallon sped across to the legside and dived – and let the ball go under his left arm. It was a deliberate miss. I reckon I was probably the only person on the ground that saw it, because I was watching Don Tallon and nobody else.'

11
LATTER YEARS

Don Tallon's success as a cricketer did not set him up for life after cricket. For one thing, he had neither the drive nor the business sense or desire to capitalise on his fame. A journalist once quoted a colleague of Tallon's as saying: 'Don's outlook is rather like an Aboriginal tribesman's. No matter how much he goes walkabout, he always finishes up with his Bundaberg tribe.' Tallon was content to live out most of his life in Bundaberg, playing club cricket there and running a corner shop. He bought his first shop in 1954 with the proceeds of his public subscription. He did move to Brisbane for a time in the 1960s, and former team-mates were taken aback to see him washing windscreens at a service station where he worked within a ball's throw of the Gabba. Tallon, probably, did not share their concern, for he never set much store by material success. He did have one indulgence: for a while he had a racehorse on lease, which raced mainly at country meetings.

According to his sister Jessie, Tallon was content with his modest, small-town life. 'He just loved Bundaberg, particularly North Bundaberg,' she said. 'This was his life: he never wanted to be anywhere else. He wasn't jealous of anybody. I never heard any remarks from him like that. He just sort of drifted along. That was his life, you know.'

On the domestic front, at least, his life was satisfying. In July 1954 at St Andrews Presbyterian Church in Bundaberg he married Lynda Kirchner, a Bundaberg woman he met at a Christmas party. It was the beginning of a happy partnership which was to last until Tallon's death. They had two daughters, Catherine, born in 1967, who became a lawyer, and Jane, born in 1972, who became performs as a cellist In Melbourne. Occasionally when cellists play vigorously, they are apt to lose their grip on their bow, which can then fly off to the side. More than once, when this happened, Jane Tallon was observed to catch the bow with her other hand before it hit the ground. It was only when someone discovered she was the daughter of Don Tallon that this was judged to be an inherited skill.

Tallon played club cricket until the late 1960s, when he was well past 50, which, if nothing else, showed his love for the game. He preferred bowling leg-breaks to keeping and regularly took 100 or more wickets a season, a few of them sensational catches off his own bowling. He was a successful batsman, too. In the first match of the 1956-57 season, for instance, he scored a century before tea (play did not begin until after lunch), the first time this had been done in Bundaberg for several seasons. As late as 1967-68, Tallon took 5 for 66 for Norths and made 41 not out in a match against his former club, Past Highs. Tallon's captain when he played for Past Highs was Noel Wright, a talented batsman. Asked why Tallon liked to bowl, Wright says: 'I think it might have been just a kind of relaxation after all his intense wicketkeeping over the years. He just loved to get that ball. Even with the new ball he'd love to have a bowl.' Wright says Tallon was just another member of the side: he never made anything of the fact he had been a Test cricketer. Indeed, Wright cannot remember him ever talking about his experiences playing big cricket.

Tom Theodore, for many years a prominent figure in Bundaberg cricket, has the same recollection. 'Donny was never a man to skite,' he says. 'He was very diffident in that way. He was a reticent type of fellow. You never got much humour out of Don. His brother Bill was very outgoing, whereas Don was quite the opposite.' Once, Colin McCool brought a team from Brisbane, including Tallon, to Bundaberg, and Tallon chose to bowl. 'The paying spectators were upset,' Theodore says. 'They wanted to see the Tallon-McCool combination. They got pretty rough about it. I was president of the local association, and I had to go and persuade Donny to change his mind. So he kept wickets, but then half-way through the innings he gave the gloves to somebody else and had a bowl.'

Tallon's father lived to witness Don's career as Australia's keeper from first to last. It was a big loss for Tallon when he died in 1957, for his father had been a dominant figure in his life. Thereafter, he relied heavily on his brother Matt, who helped set him up in a second corner shop that he ran for fifteen years before retiring in 1981. Tallon continued to suffer from stomach ulcers, a condition not helped by his enjoyment of a drink. He had another serious operation on Christmas Eve 1969, in the course of which he is said to have nearly died.

Lew Cooper, who kept wickets for Queensland off and on from the late 1950s to the late 1960s, met Tallon often but managed only once or twice to get him talking about the art of keeping. Cooper says: 'The only thing he ever said to me was that 99 per cent of nicks are on the outside edge of the bat. In other words, move your feet and take the ball on the inside of your body, particularly down the legside.' Early in the 1965-66 season, when Tallon was nearly 50, he played at the Gabba in a one-day benefit match for Ray Lindwall and Keith Miller. Cooper, who by then was Queensland's stand-in keeper, watched the match. 'I remember him stumping Keith Ziebell off a medium-pacer down the legside. It was magnificent – he had the bails off in a flash.' Tallon took ill during the match and Cooper was paged to go to the dressing room and replace him, but Tallon decided to play on.

Ziebell, the batsman Tallon stumped that day, was then on the verge of selection for Queensland. He says Len Johnson, a friend and clubmate of his, tried to bowl a full toss down the legside so he could get off the mark. In fact, the ball was of yorker length and as Ziebell tried to flick it away to leg he overbalanced, drifting momentarily out of the crease. 'The ball had hardly gone past me when the bails were off,' he says. 'I couldn't believe it.' The former Queensland batsman Jack McLaughlin, who played in the match, remembers the stumping, too. He says: 'On the day before the match I talked to Donny at the Cricketers Club. He'd had a few beers and he was obviously not with it. Anyhow, next morning, the day of the match, I got to the dressing room an hour before the game started and there was Don Tallon with his wicketkeeping gloves on, his pads on and everything. At that stage he wasn't a well man. The toss hadn't even been made, but here he was ready to go. He was a totally different man from the day before.

'I was fielding at fine leg and Donny was standing over the top of the stumps. Anyhow, Lenny Johnson bowled this ball just outside the leg stump. Ziebell went forward to play the leg glance, missed the ball completely – Tallon had the bails off in a flash. A fellow called Joe Goodwin was the umpire at square leg. I raced up and said to Joe, "I've never seen a stumping as quick as that in my life." Joe said, "Jack, it was that quick Ziebell didn't have any chance of getting his foot back. He was still going forward when the bails came off."'

Like others who played with Tallon, McLaughlin had a high opinion of Tallon's ability to read the play. During a Test at the Gabba in the 1960s McLaughlin found himself sitting next to Tallon on a balcony outside the Cricketers Club. He says: 'There was a spinner bowling – I just forget who it was – and Barry Jarman was the Australian keeper. The bowler bowled a wrong'un. As soon as he let the ball go, Tallon said to me, "He hasn't picked it," meaning Jarman. He didn't have field glasses, he was just sitting there looking through those squinty eyes of his, but he could tell before the ball had gone half-way down the pitch that Jarman hadn't picked it. I've never forgotten that.'

Various honours and invitations came Tallon's way. In 1968 he went to New Zealand as a guest speaker at a sports dinner in Hamilton, and in 1980 he was one of many former Australian players invited to London for the Centenary Test. It was later said that Tallon enjoyed the occasion so much he did not see a single ball of the match bowled. He had a variety of barley named after him, and during the Australia-England Test at the Gabba in 1982 he had a bar named after him in the Sir Leslie Wilson Stand. In 1995, long after his death, a new bridge across the Burnett River at Bundaberg was opened. It was named the Tallon Bridge.

Peter Anderson, who kept regularly for Queensland from 1986-87 to 1993-94, met Tallon, his boyhood hero, about 1974. Anderson, then about 13 years old, visited Bundaberg with a Queensland junior side. He found out where Tallon lived and went to visit him. Tallon spoke to him about keeping in an arc – that is, moving behind the stumps so that one's hands are always facing towards the stumps, like spoke in a wheel. He spoke to him about having soft hands and making sure his movements were smooth. He advised him to skip to keep himself light on his feet, as he himself had done in his youth, and to play table tennis to keep his reflexes sharp. In imitation of Tallon, Anderson never wore padded inners, the idea being that this would encourage him to develop soft hands.

A year or two before Tallon died, when he was in his mid-sixties, he played a round of golf with his daughter Jane. She was far too young to have seen him in action on the cricket field and knew of his sporting prowess by reputation only. Now, as he hit the golf ball, she glimpsed with her own eyes what she had heard so much about. Tallon had a lovely, fluent swing and hit the ball a huge distance. Watching him, Jane Tallon was able to appreciate at first hand the talent which long before had made her father famous.

Until the end of his life, Tallon still had the long, slim hands which so intrigued his team-mates in his playing days. As Doug Ring says: 'If you look at any wicketkeeper's hands you'll find almost without exception they have gnarled knuckles, bent fingers, damaged hands. Tallon had the hands of a pianist. He had long slender fingers without a mark on them. He was a freak.'

Tallon died on 7 September 1984, aged 68, after suffering a stroke. Three old cricketers who were close to him in his playing days, Ray Lindwall, Colin McCool and Bill Brown, attended the funeral. Tallon's schoolboy coach Tom O'Shea was there, too. The minister who conducted the service, Rev S J Tame, said Tallon's life had been a triumph of determination over adversity: he had reached the pinnacle of his sport despite persistent ill health. Tallon had been a gentle, humble person, he said. 'He moved among the greats and kept the common touch.' Two months later, players and spectators stood for a minute's silence in Tallon's memory during an Australia-West Indies Test at the Gabba.

12
POSTSCRIPT

If a monument were erected to Don Tallon, the inscription on it would need to say two things. The first is that, on all the available evidence, Tallon came as close as anyone in living memory to perfecting the art of wicketkeeping. The second is he was a Queenslander. Tallon's place in the history of Australian cricket must be viewed in the context of his origins: he was not only the first home-grown Queenslander to make it to the very top of the game in Australia wearing Queensland colours, but he began a Queensland tradition of wicketkeeping excellence. Three of the best Australian keepers of the 20th century were Queenslanders, and to some extent the success of the other two, Wally Grout and Ian Healy, was built on the reputation that Tallon left behind. It is interesting to find, incidentally, how highly Healy is regarded by men of Tallon's era. Arthur Morris rates Healy the second-best Australian keeper after Tallon that he has seen. Len Maddocks rates Healy and Alan Knott equal second to Tallon of all the keepers he has known from all countries.

Of Tallon, though, it can safely be said that among nearly all those who saw him in action at close quarters his supremacy is considered beyond dispute. As recently as 2000, the former English umpire Harold 'Dickie' Bird, who as a youth watched Tallon in 1948, said he still believed there had not been a better keeper. England's Godfrey Evans would have agreed. In 1984, 30 years after Tallon retired, Evans considered the matter and decided it was beyond question. He wrote of Tallon: 'He is the best keeper I have seen . . . he was most the compete wicketkeeper of all time.' Evans went on: 'Forget Knott, Marsh or Taylor; forget Engineer, Waite or Oldfield; forget Murray, Maddocks or Langley. Magnificent keepers all of them, but Don Tallon, the unobtrusive artist from Queensland, stands supreme.'

Tallon played at a time when the world's best cricketers earned next to nothing from the game. It is tempting to think he would have enjoyed playing today, when a cricketer of his stature could expect to set himself up financially for life. But the modern game might not have suited Tallon. Ken Archer, who knew him well and was personally fond of him, doubts he would have succeeded today as, say, Ian Healy has succeeded. Archer suspects Tallon may not have had either the mental resilience or the physical stamina to cope with the non-stop demands of modern, professional cricket. He was, perhaps, a man for his own time. His mate

Colin McCool summed him up: 'He was never anything but a raw-boned, woolly brained, country kid. He was also the best wicketkeeper in the world.'

STATISTICS

DONALD TALLON
Born   17 February 1916   Bundaberg, Qld
Died   7 September, 1984   Bundaberg, Qld.
Played cricket for Bundaberg, QCA Colts, Toombul, Souths, Maryborough, Qld and Australia.

FIRST CLASS CAREER

	M.	INNS.	N.O.	H.S.	RUNS	AVGE	C	S
Qld	86	153	8	193	4355	30.03	180	85
Other F.C.	10	17	3	152	630	45.00	14	10
Tours	33	32	7	116	705	28.20	58	27
Tests	21	26	3	92	394	17.13	50	8
	150	228	21	193	6034	29.14	302	130

TEST CAREER BY SEASON

TEST RECORD	YEAR	M.	INNS.	N.O.	H.S.	RUNS	AVGE	C	S
vs New Zealand	1946	1	1	–	5	5	5.00	1	1
vs England	1946-47	5	6	–	92	174	29.00	16	4
vs India	1947-48	5	5	1	37	49	12.25	11	3
vs England	1948	4	4	–	53	112	28.00	12	–
vs England	1950-51	5	8	2	18	39	6.50	8	–
vs England	1953	1	2	–	15	15	7.50	2	–
		21	26	3	92	394	17.13	50	8

TOURS
- Australian X1 to New Zealand 1946
- Australia to England   1948
- Australia to New Zealand   1949-50
- Australia to England   1953

OF INTEREST
- Don Tallon was the third youngest cricketer on debut for Queensland at 17 years, 280 days.
- When Tallon scored 193 for Queensland against Victoria in the 1935-36 season he was the youngest ever Queenslander to score a first class century. He scored his runs between lunch and tea.
- On the Australian tour of New Zealand in 1949-50, Tallon scored 116 against a New Zealand XI at Dunedin.
- For the combined XI match for Queensland and Victoria vs NSW in 1940-41, Tallon scored 109 not out in a session before lunch in a total innings of 152.
- On twelve (12) occasions he secured six (6) or more victims in a Queensland fixture.

BIBLIOGRAPHY

It's Not Over Yet: A History Of The Bundaberg Cricket Association by Nev Rackemann, Bundaberg Cricket Association, 1997

The Glovemen by Jack Pollard, Kangaroo Press, 1993

Australian Batsman From Bannerman To Harvey by A G Moyes, Harrop, 1954

Flying Stumps by Ray Lindwall, Stanley Paul & Co, 1954

Wicket Keepers Of The World by Godfrey Evans, New English Library, 1984

With England In Australia by Bruce Harris, Hutchinson's, 1947

Compton On Cricketers Past And Present by Denis Compton, Cassell, 1980

Cricket Is A Game by Colin McCool, Stanley Paul, 1961

Anything But ...An Autobiography by Richie Benaud, Hodder & Stoughton, 1998

Cricket Conquest by Bill O'Reilly, Werner Laurie, 1949

From The Boundary by Ray Robinson, Collins, 1950

Cricket At The Crossroads by Ian Johnson, Cassell, 1957

Australian Cricket Anecdotes, compiled by Gideon Haigh, Oxford University Press, 1996

Brown And Company: The Tour In Australia by Jack Fingleton, Collins, 1951

Catch! by Keith Miller and R S Whitington, Latimer House, 1951

The Gloves Are Off by Godfrey Evans, Hodder & Stoughton, 1960

Benaud On Reflection by Richie Benaud, Collins, 1984

Slasher Opens Up by Ken Mackay, Pelham Books, 1964

My Country's Keeper by Wally Grout, Pelham Books, 1965

A Century Of Cricketers by A G Moyes, Angus & Robertson, 1950

The South Africans In Australia 1952-53 by A G Moyes, Angus & Robertson, 1953

Bumper by Keith Miller and R S Whitington, Latimer House, 1953

Six And Out compiled by Jack Pollard, Pollard Publishing, 1964

Gone To The Test Match by John Arlott, Longmans, Green & Co, 1949

Elusive Victory: With F R Brown's MCC Team In Australia 1950-51 by E W Swanton, Hodder & Stoughton, 1951

Cricket Task-Force by W J O'Reilly, Werner Laurie, 1951

94 Declared: Cricket Reminiscences by Ben Travers, Elm Tree Books, 1981

Cricket Controversy by Clif Cary, Werner Laurie, 1948

On Tour With Bradman by Andy Flanagan, privately published, 1950

Testing Time For England by Denis Compton, Stanley Paul, 1947